COMPUTERS AS TUTORS

SOLVING THE CRISIS IN EDUCATION

COMPUTERS AS TUTORS

SOLVING THE CRISIS IN EDUCATION

FREDERICK BENNETT, PH.D.

PRINTED IN THE UNITED STATES OF AMERICA

Faben, Inc.
P.O. Box 3133
Sarasota, FL 34230
941-955-0050
Fax: 941-365-5472
Toll Free: 888-671-5112
E-mail: sales@fabenbooks.com
http//www.fabenbooks.com

ISBN: 0-9669583-6-5

Publisher's Cataloging-in-Publication
(Provided by Quality Books, Inc.)

Bennett, Frederick, 1928-
  Computers as tutors : solving the crisis in
education / by Frederick Bennett. –1st ed.
   p. cm.
   Includes index.
   LCCN: 99-61464
   ISBN: 0-9669583-6-5

   1. Computer-assisted instruction.
  2. Educational change–United States.
  I. Title.

LB1028.5.B46 1999   371.33'4
            QB199-69

My thanks go, above all, to Marge, who was always so helpful and supportive as this book took shape, and to whom it is dedicated.

A number of other people also offered many helpful suggestions, although they did not always agree with all my ideas. These people, in alphabetical order are Eugene Best, Isa Dempsey, David Ellison, Margaret Kemner, Bob Krescanko, and Paul Messink. To all of them also, my sincere thanks.

TABLE OF CONTENTS

PREFACE

This book has one message: schools can use technology more effectively, and for the welfare of students, teachers and society, they must do so.

Businesses and other organizations throughout the world have made gigantic strides as a result of better applications of technology. Schools, despite their acquisition of millions of computers, waddle along as they have for eons. They waste the power of these machines and reap negligible educational benefits as shown by the lack of improvement in overall test scores. Meanwhile, fervent pleas from parents for improved schools result in verbal agreement from educators and politicians, but no effective action follows. This dialogue has continued for years. The difficulties in education remain virtually untouched. Hope of major improvements under present conditions is little more than a fantasy.

Today's technology, if used differently, could bring advances that would improve education dramatically. Ordinary students would make massive gains and restraints on bright students would dissolve. Wherever illiteracy is a problem, it would be eliminated, and handicapped students would have immense new vistas opened to them. If computers are to be effective in schools, however, overthrowing present practices must occur, and that frightens many people. Opposition is therefore inevitable. Some human instructors will object emotionally, fearing that more extensive employment of technology will seriously degrade their position. Their trepidation is understandable but groundless. Although teachers will have to alter their accustomed practices, they will reach a new level of importance, will accomplish more, and will have greater job satisfaction when schools take advantage of the power of computers. Some parents may also object to technology fearing that an Orwellian world will engulf their children. This fear is also false. Computerized education, properly used, can provide a personal side to education that is impossible today.

Despite the present retarded pace of change in schools, a real revolution can happen. Compelling evidence of the power of effective computerized education is available in a few places. When parents become aware of this evidence, and when they become cognizant of what computers can do under still better conditions, they, together with other concerned citizens, can force schools to use computers properly. Schooling will become both enjoyable for children and supremely effective. Thereafter, the dire weakness of much of today's education will vanish.

This book explains why computers have failed to alter education until now, how they should be employed, and the startling advances their appropriate use will bring. I am a psychologist and rely on principles of that science to support the arguments favoring improved use of these machines. I am also a professional computer programmer and apply knowledge acquired in that role to show the gains that technology can bring to education—gains that may seem like fantasies to anyone who hasn't studied the power and capability of this technology. Although I am an American and stress the difficulties in schools in the United States, computers can remake and improve education throughout the world.

Effective computerization in education will happen eventually, simply because the advantages are monumental. Nonetheless, the longer the change is delayed, the more present students are deprived of the benefits that could accrue to them. The necessary prerequisite for this change to occur is thorough discussion by educators, parents, politicians, and concerned individuals of what can and should be done. This book attempts to hasten this process.

Computers can remake education. It is time to begin.

A WARNING

AND

PROPOSED

SOLUTIONS

Chapter 1

The Warning

*J*ames Bryant Conant was a scholar whose talents extended over a wide range of activities. He was a scientist, writer, and dedicated citizen. Harvard University selected him to be its president, and he filled that position for twenty years. In 1953, President Eisenhower sent him to Germany, first as High Commissioner, and two years later, as American Ambassador. After returning to the United States in 1957, he devoted most of the years until his death in 1978 studying, writing, and agonizing about the nation's educational system. In 1961, appalled by the poor education he found in American inner cities, he warned that "social dynamite" was accumulating.[1]

Politicians and educators effectively ignored his dire assessment. They did nothing. Within five years after Conant published his frightening insight, events established him as a prophet. The inner cities exploded in devastating riots.

The destruction shocked the nation, but the response of authorities was meaningless and has continued that way after each subsequent occurrence. Whenever riots erupt in the cities, an almost ritualistic series of events takes place. First, astonishment and horror overwhelm America. Loud but indefinite cries rise quickly, insisting that the government must do something— anything. These demands are unanswered, but an interlude without riots follows. During those pacific periods the American public quickly forgets, imagining the disturbances were temporary phenomena that won't be repeated. Then the destruction happens again in another upheaval. Despite the absolute accuracy of Conant's foresight, leaders and officials continue to ignore what he saw as the underlying and precipitating cause of the destructive force: lack of education.

The riots are only one effect of the social dynamite that continues to accumulate. Rampant crime, which terrorizes the nation is another. This lawlessness often comes into mainstream America. Consequently, it enrages and exasperates the citizens more than the riots in the inner cities. Citizens fear for their safety. They plead for solutions, but officials can only proffer trite and anemic answers: more police, additional arrests, longer sentences, added prisons. Seldom does anyone in authority address the criminal activity–poor education connection. Jonathan Kozol in *Illiterate America* pointed out that illiteracy and imprisonment are directly linked,[2] and statistics from across the nation bear him out. For example, in Florida 43 percent of state-prison inmates test below the sixth grade level,[3] and math skills of 65 percent of New York prisoners don't meet eighth grade standards.[4] Twenty-five million adults, more than the entire population of the state of New York, are functionally illiterate.

If the impossible were accomplished, and the government apprehended and confined all felons, the nation would quickly replace them. Another huge group of illiterates will leave school this year, and next year, and every year thereafter. Unable to compete in a technological society, many will choose crime. Although not the only element in lawlessness, illiteracy and its cause, substandard schooling, must be confronted before criminal activity is controlled.

If further confirmation of the debacle flowing from inferior education were needed, welfare problems provide abundant proof. A Ford Foundation study found that almost 60 percent of the out-of-wedlock births by young women occurred among those who scored in the lowest 20 percent on a basic-skills test.[5] Obviously, poor learning must also be addressed before finding an answer to welfare reform. The government talks about trying to educate welfare recipients to help them escape from the debilitating system. Usually, that is too late. They could have been and should have been educated before they got into their present predicament.

Even when rioting, crime, or welfare isn't involved, abysmal education is costly. Many major companies carry on expensive programs to provide basic education for their employees. In 1991 the *New York Times* bemoaned that "business has become America's second-largest educator. It now spends a record forty billion dollars a year on education, about three-quarters of this to teach workers basic skills they should have learned in school".[6]

Since legions of students require remedial education, many youths obviously spend their formative years in schools without becoming educated. Inferior schooling affects the least learned but also taints those who plan to go to college. The federal government reported in 1989 that 21 percent of college freshmen were enrolled in remedial math classes, 16 percent were studying remedial writing and at least 13 percent were taking remedial reading.[7] Despite the emphasis on improving education, six years later these figures showed little change. In the fall of 1995, 29 percent of first-time freshmen enrolled in at least one remedial reading, writing, or mathematics course.[8]

Over the past several years there have been several tests given that compared students throughout the world. Americans consistently ranked very low, even though the test takers often did not include students from other advanced nations such as Japan, Germany, or England.

In 1998 a new study was released. This was the Third International Mathematics and Science Study (TIMSS), which looked at pupils in the final year of secondary school. Again, the U.S. ranked in the lowest quarter out of twenty-one nations in Mathematics and Science Achievement. This time, none of the Asian nations participated. The educator who coordinated the American portion of the study, William Schmidt, of Michigan State University was quoted as saying "Our best students in mathematics and science are simply not world class. Even the very small percentage of students taking advanced placement courses are not among the world's best." President Bill Clinton was obviously shocked. He said "There is something wrong with the system and it is our generation's responsibility to fix it. You cannot blame the schoolchildren. There is no excuse for this." [9]

This poor showing of American education has been going on for years. In an article in *The New Republic*, January 6, 1984, entitled "Japan's Smart Schools" Diane Ravitch who is a historian of education and noted author in the field wrote, "The average high school graduate in Japan is said to be as well educated as the average college graduate in the United States." A study by Harold Stevenson maintained that, "by the fifth grade, the worst Japanese class in the study was ahead of the best American class[10]."

The weakness of American students is evident not only when contrasted with other nations but also when compared with American pupils of other times.

Scholastic Aptitude Test (SAT) scores have declined in recent years. Although many authorities shudder at this reduction,[11] some educators blithely dismiss the results. They declare lower scores come about because the number of SAT test takers has expanded, and the tests have become more democratic. Even these educational Pollyannas can't explain why 1991 Scholastic Aptitude Test scores of entering freshmen at prestigious colleges had also declined markedly.[12] This is shocking, especially since it accompanies an intense national disquietude about education.

Effects of poor education always show wide-reaching effects. The government issued a report in July of 1991, about skills that are needed "to hold a decent job and earn a decent living."[13] Labor Secretary Lynn Martin complained that "more than half of young people leaving high school won't have the knowledge or foundation required to achieve either goal."[14]

Lack of education even haunts workers with a job and hinders their full enjoyment of working. The Dow Jones News Service carried an article that pointed out problems of one worker at a major American corporation.

> Jimmy Wedmore, a General Motors Corp. hourly worker, used to run from promotions. Wedmore couldn't read or write and was afraid he'd be discovered if he advanced beyond his job on the assembly line here. "Better jobs kept coming and I had to keep turning them down," says Wedmore, age 50. "It's really a pitiful situation to be in." Finally, he asked for help. In 1986, GM provided a tutor who taught him to read, write and solve basic math problems. Wedmore, who used to assemble parts for starter motors, now runs a high-tech machine that produces powder used to make powerful magnets. "I love the challenge of this job," he says. "You learn something new every day."[15]

Jimmy Wedmore finally got an education that enabled him to lead a more satisfying life. Lamentably, he had to struggle through many flawed years deprived of what he should have had when he finished school. The years of success he had at General Motors prove that he was able to learn while in school. Wasting those years without education was unfortunate for Jimmy Wedmore. Losing the talents of armies of Jimmy Wedmores who are being jettisoned from schools today with an inferior education is a deplorable waste for society.

If nothing else, the educational disaster in America has drawn powerful comments. In 1983, the National Commission on Excellence in Education complained, "If an unfriendly nation had attempted to impose upon America the mediocre educational performance that exists today, we might well have viewed it as an act of war."[16] The same Commission quoted analyst Paul Copperman when he grieved that:

> Each generation of Americans has outstripped its parents in education, in literacy, and in economic attainment. For the first time in the history of our country, the educational skills of one generation will not surpass, will not equal, will not even approach those of their parents.[17]

It seems apparent that education in the United States is in a calamitous condition. On occasion, calamities can lead to massive changes because they stimulate profound reactions. In 1775 the English Parliament created monumental difficulties for the Colonists who then revolted. The original adversity caused a new nation to arise. The present educational crisis could galvanize the nation and bring an educational revolution that will turn the present catastrophe into a stunning triumph. A century from now civilization will judge if the educational distress in America in the last years of the twentieth century led ultimately to profound improvement of schools, or to more terrible consequences.

Chapter 2

Some Suggested Solutions

*T*he crisis has caught the attention of many leaders in the United States who talk of a need for a revolutionary approach to solve the problems. Those supposed "revolutions" are replete with good intentions but few radical ideas. President Bush and his administration introduced a program called *AMERICA 2000*. Considerable fanfare accompanied its debut. The objective was superb: revitalize education completely by the year 2000. Even this proposal with its grandiose goals hesitated to suggest radical solutions. It stated early in the document, "few elements of this strategy are unprecedented."[1]

Educators seldom propose any serious change for schools. While they readily admit the problems are intense, many feel it will be sufficient to leave the present educational system in place while making minor revisions. This reluctance to embrace difficult changes is a standard response to a crisis. Many honest and upstanding citizens in the American colonies wanted to solve the problem of taxation without representation by less drastic means than revolution. Today, many honest and upstanding leaders of the country follow a similar path. They dismiss serious disruptions that will accompany a genuine revolution in education as impractical and unnecessary.

Although substantive changes are avoided, the difficulties with schooling keep gnawing at the American psyche. Many possible answers have been advanced, and some that have gotten national attention require comment here.

Increased Funding

One solution, commonly proposed, is to call for more money for education. This demand is neither new nor guaranteed to produce noteworthy results.

Funding for education in the United States increased approximately 33 percent in real terms from 1980 to 1990. Nonetheless, during that decade, noticeable improvement in American schools was lacking.

Perhaps an argument can be made that increased funding might help if it were wisely applied, but the horrendous problems inherent in education today would remain. Advocates recommend increased funding for various reasons. Sometimes they contend more dollars will buy additional computers, and education, astride modern technology, will leap over its current barriers. I will explain in Chapters 7 and 8 why more computers alone will add little to what millions of computers are accomplishing now: virtually nothing.

Another reason for seeking additional funding is the supposed benefits that would accrue if schools could raise salaries of teachers. Additional pay, advocates contend, would bring the cream of American students into teaching and improve schools. Additional pay hasn't helped thus far. The increased funding of the 1980s brought better compensation for teachers, but the quality of students entering the profession did not improve appreciably. Teachers, today, have an aggravating and difficult job. Consequently, many are unhappy in their positions, and morale is often low. A poll of two thousand teachers in 1989 conducted by Louis Harris and Associates illustrates how teachers view themselves. The results revealed only 53 percent of respondents felt they were respected by society, and only 67 percent would advise a young person to go into teaching.[2] Although higher pay might lessen these difficulties, morale involves much more than pay. Further monetary increases will not guarantee a supply of upper tier students for education while low morale brought on by teaching conditions remains.

Moreover, schools must compete with industry when they recruit certain classes of teachers. Math and science instructors are crucial but are in short supply. School systems have difficulty paying wages for these teachers that private industry won't surpass. Even if school boards were to decree that everybody with a math or science degree would receive a substantial pay raise, industry, which also needs these people, would increase their own salary levels. Math and science teachers would continue in an inferior pay position compared with industry. Of course, conditions in education exacerbate the problem of insufficient math and science majors. Poor education prevents the development of many potential scientists. This problem probably begins in grade school. Most elementary teachers are uncomfortable teaching science.[3]

The results from educational districts without excessive monetary shortfalls also bring into question the contention that more funding would drastically alter education. Students entering prestigious universities often come from these better-funded districts. If these districts were providing superlative education, SAT scores for those entering the more highly rated universities would be rising, or at least, not declining. The conclusion must be that merely pouring more dollars into the problem will not solve it.

Copy Other Nations

Some authorities propose another seemingly less difficult solution: study schools of other nations and then imitate what they are doing. The divergence in test scores noted above shows that educational results in many other nations are better than in the United States. If America mimics what others are doing, a drastic overhaul of American education will not be necessary.

Other nations are using the same basic system that was successful in the United States for many years. Education in America fails to achieve the results of former times because the nation has changed. Part of the altered climate is due to the underlying social structure. Public officials and private commentators often decry lessened family standards in the country. Concerned educators legitimately bewail the home conditions of many of their students. They make the valid argument that a return to the life in America of twenty-five or fifty years ago would improve education. They particularly deplore lessened participation of parents in school programs and less parental direction of children. Anyone who studies schooling in America must agree: more involvement of guardians would help to produce better education.

Parents, however, are unlikely to make a sudden turnabout. Trying to return to previous times is an attempt to stop another societal upheaval. Those who struggle against ongoing changes in society have met a string of failures. Even religions, which have always exercised a strong influence in the nation, have been unsuccessful. For example, some years ago when many priests and ministers vociferously decried the trend of more businesses staying open Sunday, they didn't stop a developing change. Today, stores are open throughout America every Sunday. Religions have seen the futility of their struggle and have accepted the inevitable.

Teachers do more than utter complaints about the problems. They also strive to change conditions. Nonetheless, they make little progress. Many parents, especially those who are alone, can't hold a full time job, run a household of never ending responsibilities, and still create the additional time to be as active in the education of their children as they might wish. This situation is truly unfortunate, but bemoaning it won't change it.

Part of the present condition stems from the change in the basic idea of "family" in the United States. The idealized couple of Ozzie and Harriet where the wife stayed home, and the husband alone supplied the livelihood has gone. It won't return. Demographics in the United States today have changed. For example, single mothers are raising fifteen million children. Even in two parent families, both parents often work outside the home. Sometimes the income of one is insufficient, and both must be employed. Women also work because they find it enjoyable and challenging to participate in the commercial world, and they can hire domestic help. Whatever the reasons, many parents fail to take the active role in the schoolwork of their children that educators seek. Schools must encourage this participation, but with society seemingly headed in a different direction, merely waiting for the trend to stop will not solve the current educational problems.

Another powerful reason why copying other systems won't suffice is because the United States encompasses a more pluralistic society than any other nation. Immigration built America's population, and the influx continues today. The government predetermines that many thousands of immigrants from individual countries may take up residence in the United States every year. In addition, citizens of other nations who are experiencing political repression can seek and obtain permission to enter. This inflow increases the yearly immigration totals by hundreds of thousands. It doesn't stop there, of course. Millions of illegal immigrants now reside in the nation, and hundreds or thousands more pour in every day. As a result of these new arrivals, 8 percent of those living in the United States in 1992 were born in another nation, and those figures are rising.

These rivers of immigration bring huge numbers of new students that descend upon schools. Frequently, immigrants are poorly educated. Often they can't speak English. They come from a multitude of customs, languages, and backgrounds. No nation, other than the United States, has a similar condition. No existing educational system tries to cope with such an ongoing influx of new residents.

Another obstacle prevents the importation of approaches of other nations: the heritage of slavery in this country. When Emancipation took place, black children were far behind academically. For decades after the nation abolished slavery, America was able to hide from itself results of involuntary servitude. The "separate but equal" system of education provided camouflage. The deplorable educational condition of former slaves was continued for their children by a segregated and inferior school system. Residual effects throttle the nation even today. Schools in America must struggle to counteract a legacy that doesn't burden other nations.

The conclusion must be that copying methods of other countries can't provide the answers.

"Choice"

Another proposed solution today is "Choice," under which parents could choose the school their children attend. Under one form, parents could choose only among public schools. A variation would permit parents to opt for either public or private schools. If the Choice option were adopted that allows selection of private schools, the government would help parents pay for any schooling, but private schools would usually require additional payment. Poor parents would still be forced to choose public schools. The ultimate result would be public schools filled with more impoverished students who most need better schooling. Financing for public schools would also be lessened because all students would eventually become eligible for assistance, including those of parents who now opt and pay for private schools. There would be less money per pupil for public schools.

Arguments for and against Choice abound. It seems likely that it might benefit parents who have sufficient resources to send their children to the better private schools. Nonetheless, by itself with nothing additional, it can't change education sufficiently to make American children equal to youth of other nations in learning. One weakness of this approach is evident by returning again to private schools where sufficient funds are available today. Thousands of schools today operate under the basic idea of the right of a parent to choose a school for their children to attend. Many have greater endowments and income than can be expected in new schools that would exist under Choice. Students from these private schools often score better on standardized tests than students from public schools. No evidence, however, proves that most students from these private schools can equal students from other nations. Even with Choice, schools would be unable to provide individualized tutoring, a help for bright students but crucial for students who are behind. Raising enough money for this type of instruction in today's schools is unthinkable.

In any discussion of Choice another element is important: public schools have difficulties unknown in private schools. For example, public schools cannot be selective since every student must be offered an education somewhere. Public schools must also teach learning-disabled and special-education pupils, and this often increases costs. Opponents of Choice also fear that better students will flee the public schools leaving behind only the poorest students, whose education will be even worse than now. This would be a destructive happening because the biggest crisis in American schools today is among these students. It is difficult to imagine that private organizations will make a meaningful effort to build and operate many schools in the inner cities.

A subtle yet deleterious aspect of the present debate about Choice is that many dedicated and influential people expend their efforts to bring about Choice as if it alone would solve the problems. It won't. Even if it improved parts, the basic deficiencies would remain. When these leaders devote their abilities and influence primarily to encouraging Choice, they cannot employ their full energies to revolutionize education in America.

The Internet

Another proposed solution arises from the profound changes that the Internet is bringing to many areas. I am a devoted user of the Internet and believe that it will have dramatic effects in the world beyond anything we can now imagine. Nonetheless, as a means of revolutionizing education, I believe it falls far short of what proponents seem to be hoping.

Unfortunately, the attraction of the Internet as a solution is often that it can apparently be imposed merely on top of the present system and not create any real disturbance. Merely add wiring to schools, some machines and modems, and presto, education will necessarily improve. A closer look at the World Wide Web or Internet shows the fallacy of this position.

The Internet has two major functions: it is a superb library with features that cannot be duplicated by any other means, and it is also an outstanding means of communication. Let me pose a hypothetical question: Would it be possible to take the children and set them down in libraries and expect them to become educated? The answer is obvious. Even though a few of the brightest might profit from the experience, even these outstanding children would waste considerable time and energy before achieving any real learning. Children, especially, need structure.

A library can be extremely valuable as a learning tool if the child can first learn how to use the library and can be taught the fundamentals of doing research. That is the role of education. This is the first difficulty with the Internet. It is, in effect, a massive library with many spectacular features, but still a library.

The other side to the Internet is its capacity for communication across the world, a feature that will prove to be of incstimable value. Nonetheless, it is not a practical primary tool with which to educate children. Lack of structure is again the villain. Although children might theoretically communicate with many learned people, there are only so many learned people. Most students will spend the bulk of their time communicating with those who are less than learned, just as most students (and most adults also) spend more time reading less than the most learned journals. The Internet can and will be a valuable tool in education. I will mention some of its uses later when I speak of seminars and workshops in Chapter 19. Nonetheless, the Internet, by itself, will not provide the revolution needed today.

Conclusion

None of these proposed solutions will change the nation's educational system into one that will suddenly revitalize learning. Nonetheless, the need to remake education is arguably the preeminent problem in the United States, as it is in all nations, because children everywhere must be educated for a rapidly changing and increasingly technological world. Effective answers must be discovered. New educational methods, superior to older ones and easily duplicated, must be developed. The Office of Technology Assessment has summarized this crisis saying:

> American education is at a crucial juncture. The demands on schooling in our pluralistic society are greater than they have ever been. An increasing percentage of students are educationally at risk, and demographic projections make clear that this problem will continue to grow. In addition, schools must prepare all young people with a new set of skills and understandings to assure the Nation's economic competitiveness.[4]

Opponents of serious reform in any area, including education, are seldom satisfied by evidence that a radical new method is efficient. They continually demand more proof. No advocate of retaining today's system suggests, however, that current educational practices must prove that they are effective. A cursory glance at today's dilemmas makes it obvious that proof like that would be difficult to find. Education is in a troubled state. Teachers are not at fault. They try valiantly to help students by supporting a system that cannot cope with the vast changes erupting in the world. These teachers, although unhappy with results, cannot remake education and eliminate the horrendous problems, or they would have done it.

Only a revolution could have sufficed to cause the truly dramatic changes that resulted in the formation of the American nation in 1776. Only a real revolution will bring the turnabout needed to revitalize education today. Unfortunate side effects, however, accompany revolutions. Before the upheaval is concluded, a number of people suffer. This happened in the American Revolution. The needed shock in schooling will also be wrenching for some educators unless they bring themselves to embrace different methods. For millions of pupils, however, failure to make changes will intensify and worsen the current crisis.

SECTION II

SEARCHING
FOR A
TRUE
SOLUTION

Chapter 3

A Look at Education

*D*eveloping suitable answers for today's school dilemmas requires an examination of the essentials of education. Whenever an attempt is made to institute any profound change, a disguised danger hides as efforts begin. Authorities responsible for developing a new direction may believe it necessary to continue whatever is being done if it has an extensive history. Scrutiny of basics will provide a foundation for a true overhaul and will show what can be changed, if necessary, and what must be kept intact.

Education involves transference to others of knowledge and values accumulated by humans, and the development of skills allowing students to integrate this knowledge and those values into their lives. Schools and teachers have been part of education for hundreds or even thousands of years. Everyone, however, has gained knowledge outside school. We learn through experience, by watching others and by viewing television and movies. Academic learning has always taken place without teachers through books. For example, Abraham Lincoln studied law by reading at home.

Since learning has happened without schools and without teachers, neither schools nor teachers must be considered as indispensable despite their long use. Modern technology could probably eliminate them, and authorities should first examine their weaknesses and strengths. Even if society decides to retain either or both, fundamental changes may be possible and beneficial.

Schools

Present shortcomings of schools are notably evident in large American inner-city institutions where learning is difficult or impossible. Syndicated columnist Ann Landers printed a letter from a teacher in Philadelphia on May 3, 1992. The teacher complained:

> At least half of the students arrive late. It is such a common occurrence that nothing is said. There is a constant level of noise throughout the building. It is more like a lunatic asylum than a place of learning. As I fight my way to the classroom, I try to avoid being knocked down by someone who is running, fighting, looking to start trouble or just being obnoxious.... At least 50 percent of the students in this place carry a weapon.... There is an awful lot of lawlessness here because kids don't care about suspension, detention or grades.... Our schools need help and they need it now.

This letter summarizes problems faced by schools where external conditions disrupt learning. Psychological impediments exacerbate the physical difficulties of schools. Youths are particularly influenced by peer pressure. This often prevents students from excelling in studies. As an educational conference noted:

> Peer pressure profoundly influences the academic behavior of students. By the time students reach their teens, peer groups may actually define the stance most of them take toward academic achievement and effort. Typically, peer pressure motivates students to stay in school and graduate, but even as they frown on failure, peers also restrain high achievement.... Some student cultures actively reject academic aspirations. In this case, high grades can be a source of peer ridicule and when effort is hostage to peer pressure, those high achievers who persist anyway may face strong social sanctions.[1]

This adverse effect often happens in inner-city schools but may occur elsewhere. I will later discuss the difficulty that female students may encounter in certain subjects like science and math.

Unquestionably, schools as they are now constituted have many weaknesses. They also have, however, valuable and constructive effects:

1. Schools enable students to interact with each other, and this is an important element in growing up and in learning.

2. Schools also furnish structure and can provide a means for ensuring that students devote time to necessary studies.
3. Under proper circumstances, schools can foster peer pressure to aid learning.
4. If schools were eliminated, the probable alternative would be to have education take place in homes of students. Although home schooling is advantageous for some children, conditions in the homes of others would impede learning.

Since schools provide advantages that can assist education, they should remain. Nonetheless, mere cosmetic adjustments in schools can't rectify the problems. The serious drawbacks of schools obstruct learning and demand extensive changes.

Teachers

Like schools, teachers have disadvantages and advantages. Their negative features are easily overlooked since teachers are universally accepted in education, and almost everybody had a favorite teacher. Nonetheless, present teaching has serious problems that any potential reform must evaluate and address.

Students have many teachers during their schooling. While adults may cherish the memory of an extraordinary teacher who aided them, they don't remember many in this way. By definition, few people of exceptional caliber exist in any profession. Besides a shortage of sensational teachers, some are decidedly inferior. This has always been true, but every poor instructor impedes learning and makes school unpleasant and difficult.

Another disadvantage of teachers flows from the ingrained attitudes they carry with them when they enter classrooms. This preset disposition sometimes is detrimental. In an article generally favorable toward teachers, J. R. Dusek summarizes existing research. He concludes:

> evidence indicating that teachers form expectations for students' performance is abundant.... [and] teachers tend to treat students differently depending on their expectations for the students' performance.... [and] these expectancies, and presumably their behavioral manifestations, have been shown to relate to students' academic achievement.[2]

Nobody has ever suggested a viable means of changing this perplexity.

Conditions in their classrooms, not their abilities or attitudes, present the foremost difficulty for teachers. They cannot devote their full attention to each student individually, but they must teach diverse students simultaneously. Anyone wishing to convey knowledge as each student could ideally receive it, is thwarted. Brighter students can quickly grasp the lesson while slower students are still struggling to understand. Teachers must make decisions about how fast to go. Even if higher authorities decide how much must be taught, some students will fail to progress as far as they are able. Others will fail to reach even minimally acceptable standards.

Teachers also suffer from the usual human stresses of sickness, accidents, psychological problems, boredom, and burnout. Just as they lessen results in other professions, these impairments hinder teaching and result in poorer learning by students. Sometimes these impediments remove instructors from their classrooms. Regular teachers are then replaced by substitutes who are unfamiliar with the classes. An entire chapter, later in the book, is necessary to address this debilitating problem.

As with most human beings, teachers can be slow to change. Although evidence exists that modern technology at times can aid teaching, relatively few instructors employ it in their classrooms. Also, research findings are often ignored.

These are negative characteristics of instructors that impede learning. Teachers, however, have many strong traits that can enhance education immensely:

1. In the lives of their students, teachers often achieve an influence beyond the intellectual knowledge they impart. Adults often look back on a teacher who had a stirring and positive effect upon their lives.

2. Human teachers can make decisions that might be difficult for a machine. For example, a computer can judge grammatical integrity in a paper, but evaluating the worth of original ideas is impossible for today's machines.

3. Many teachers are extraordinarily creative and develop new and better ways of teaching.

4. By their presence, teachers stress that learning must be integrated into a world populated by intelligent and feeling beings.

5. Teachers, helping students to understand and accept each other, can ease interpersonal problems that often develop.
6. Teachers can be role models that children need.

Summation

Schools have both positive and negative features for education, and teachers also have benefits and shortcomings. An effective revolution in education will need to revamp schools and the role of teachers by discarding or lessening present weaknesses and failings, while retaining and amplifying their strengths.

Chapter 4
Pleasure in Learning

*A*nother important component of a true solution must be considered and should be incorporated, if it can be done. Learning should be enjoyable. The reason for this is more than just a foolish wish. The quest for this enjoyment is founded in human nature.

Newborn children are soon hungry and curious. They want to eat, and they want to learn about their surroundings. They suckle at the breast, and they swivel their heads toward sounds. When they can see, they stare at anything new. Eating and learning both carry out innate needs or desires that drive humans throughout their lives. A rule of nature requires that actions fulfilling innate desires be pleasurable. Without enjoyment, necessary actions would cease, and the species would die out. This pleasure is obvious and well understood for eating. The enjoyment stemming from the innate desire to learn is often overlooked.

Despite the inherent satisfaction of actions that meet basic needs, other conditions may interfere with the usual pleasure. Researchers studying behavior of white rats sometimes combine tasty food with an electrical shock at a certain place in the cage. If the rat nibbles at food in that area, it will be shocked, and it doesn't take the rat long to avoid eating there. If an animal refuses to eat good food in a specific location, that area must be responsible. Students should enjoy their classes because learning is the object. If children are unhappy with schooling, the circumstances or the place may be the cause, but something is wrong.

Millions of children openly express their dislike for formal education. Many drop out. Others remain and attend classes but are bored. When animals or humans don't find healthy food in appropriate conditions, they look elsewhere for nourishment to satisfy their basic need. When students don't find suitable learning in appropriate conditions, they also look elsewhere. They satisfy the fundamental desire to learn by finding other sources like TV, their peers, and movies where learning is pleasurable as it should be. If this "education" replaces what they should receive in school, they and society both suffer. Valuable and available stores of accumulated knowledge are unused and replaced by junk learning, just as animals or humans might be forced to eat junk food when the good food is in a location where eating is painful. Although reasons abound why education may be unpleasant, some are especially critical:

1. Schools must bind students in a rigid mold where they have to receive instruction at the same pace as twenty to thirty others, all with different capabilities and interests.

2. Monotonous and uninteresting classes repel students and make it unpleasant to learn. Like everyone else, you, the reader, can remember when you were forced at times during your schooling, to endure tedious classes. Unfortunately, teachers without special talents, despite their sincere efforts, may provide classes that overwhelm the inherent enjoyment of learning.

3. Students with poorer grades, who account for many serious rejections of education, confront a continuous series of frustrations. They quickly get behind in the early grades and never catch up. Being behind, they lack a real opportunity to learn and miss the chance to enjoy formal education. School becomes a grating, despised activity.

4. Brighter students have different barriers interfering with their learning, but often they also find education unpleasant. The system bores them and fails to challenge them. Although learning new material brings them enjoyment, their delight diminishes when the pace is tiresome. Again, teachers are guiltless. If they go fast enough to make education completely satisfying for brighter children, they interfere with the learning of others.

5. Teaching to the exact ability of diverse students is utterly impossible without individual tutors. Enjoyable learning requires that instruction meet the intellectual capacity of each student just as food must meet individual needs in each animal.

Education of students with unequal levels of ability in the same class, with some teachers who lack stimulating approaches, has been going on for centuries. Pupils have been able to learn despite these shortcomings. Many do so under these same handicaps today, but this learning does not prove the efficacy of the educational system. It only emphasizes the strength of the innate drive that enables people to acquire knowledge in spite of obstacles. Nonetheless, when lack of learning and boredom are rife in schools, youngsters often revolt against the educational process. Their antics create havoc within schools and obstruct learning for themselves and for others. Unfortunately, the usual reaction is to blame students. This scapegoating of pupils is equivalent to blaming animals that refuse to eat in a place where they have discovered they will receive an electric shock.

If pupils enjoyed their schools and their education, their learning would improve and much of their current rebellion against the system would dissipate. Fewer discipline problems in schools would be an immediate result. Authorities would then be able to devote more of their time and resources to improving education instead of merely holding it together. Making the time that children spend in school more enjoyable is a key element in the needed revolution in learning.

Chapter 5

A True Solution

When Patrick Koch of Parma, Ohio, was a second grader, his parents bought him an expensive new encyclopedia. His mother and father quickly forgot the cost when Patrick liked the new books and began to read them with enthusiasm. After a few sessions poring over his new learning tool, Patrick announced one morning that he was not going to school. He felt he could learn more by reading his encyclopedia than by attending his ordinary classes. His parents rejected this innovative plan of learning, and the youngster again headed to the classroom. His parents weren't unduly conservative. Rarely would guardians trust their child's education to a novel experiment in self-instruction. They would fear that instead of helping him, it might hinder his education.

Members of school boards are sometimes confronted with suggested changes in schools, and they often feel like Patrick's parents. New proposals might not improve education but might only degrade it further. Board members who must periodically face reelection cringe at the prospect of an unexpected blunder outraging voters. They usually select a safe course and rely on the opinions of their experts: teachers and school officials. This further slows the onset of new programs because educators usually don't relish major changes. Like most of us, they prefer familiar methods.

Sometimes schools can embrace new approaches because they aren't controversial. School boards have discovered one major innovation that fits this requirement: they have added millions of computers to their schools. Parents applaud this change. They feel computers must be good for schools since they are modern, and intelligent people outside schools use them everywhere. Teachers don't object either when these new machines are added. Those who want to employ computers to help them teach have the machines available, while most instructors can ignore them, and nobody will force their use. Administrators aren't threatened because the computers won't bring any substantial change in the way they operate their schools. Computers are, therefore, a rare innovation: they please everybody. Modern machines are in place; this pleases parents. Traditional education undergoes no real upheaval; this pleases teachers and administrators. A new undertaking isn't controversial; this pleases school boards. Unfortunately for students, under present conditions computers don't make much difference in their learning. Education remains unchanged and frequently impoverished.

Occasionally, someone comes along who suggests that computers ought to be used differently, even perhaps to do what has always been done by human instructors: to teach. Whenever this occurs, school authorities find themselves in the position of Patrick's parents when he advanced his unexpected idea. Teachers have always taught in schools and therefore, their position is considered essential and unchangeable. The suggestion of using computers in a way that might infringe upon activities of teachers is akin to the child suggesting the encyclopedia as a replacement for classes. A major difference, however, separates the encyclopedic learning that fascinated the second grader, and expanded use of computer learning, which fascinates students. Patrick's method has never been tried. Computers, however, without teachers in their customary roles, have educated students. Results of programs using computers in this way can be examined to discover whether a radical new use of these machines is truly practical.

At-Risk Students

Computers have been used extensively without traditional teaching with "at-risk" students. Why computers have been able to penetrate education with this group requires an explanation of previous failed attempts to cope with a difficult challenge.

Every year, sizable numbers of students leave school without graduation and before they reach an age when they should no longer be in high school. These are school dropouts. An increase in the dropout rate of a school system frightens officials because something is obviously askew. It also raises a glaring target for critics. Therefore, keeping students in classrooms has become a compelling goal for school authorities. Besides avoiding criticism, administrators may gather a few laurels by retaining these students. Authorities can figure the percentage of their students who drop out and can contrast results with percentages lost by their schools in other years. If their numbers are favorable, they can allow and encourage a comparison of their figures with those of other school systems. The media often become involved. Results are publicized in local newspapers and by radio and TV stations. Sometimes statistics from notable systems like New York City may be publicized nationally. If a dropout rate is decreasing, schools trumpet the news. The drive to hold students in school even arouses state legislatures. Some have passed laws decreeing that students who drop out prematurely cannot have licenses to drive automobiles while their classmates remain in school.

A mystique has grown up in education about lessening the number of dropouts. A reduction is assumed to signify schools are making important advances in their battle to turn education around. This assumption is blatantly false for many children. These are the hordes of youngsters who want to drop out because they haven't been successful in school, haven't been able to learn during their many years of attending. Their previous record makes it unlikely much improvement will result by future attendance. Simply retaining children in classes can't solve the educational dilemmas of students or schools, because learning does not necessarily accompany attendance. Nonetheless, schools brag about their diminished dropout rates as if they were actually making significant progress. If a lower rate is accompanied by a different approach in educating the students, it can be meaningful. If it only means retaining students in a system that has consistently failed to educate them, nothing is accomplished.

Since schools are anxious to retain their potential dropouts, they try to identify them early and to target them with specific programs. They label pupils who are likely to leave prematurely as "at-risk" students.

Schools have developed ways to locate these at-risk students. Usually their poor scholastic record and their negative attitude toward school assist in identifying them. One school system describes a typical at-risk student, and thus a potential candidate for a dropout-prevention program, as one who "appears uninterested in school and is generally apathetic toward school as evidenced by tardiness, truancy, and low grades."

After finding at-risk students, school systems establish goals for their programs by setting a retention rate they deem acceptable under their conditions. For example, a system might set the goal of keeping 60 percent of identified potential dropouts in school. If this aim were reached, the program would be considered effective. Ordinarily, no further objectives would be established. Educating these students is seldom a specified goal. Rarely would anyone expect students who were woefully deficient after about a decade in schools to change suddenly and become stellar students.

All systems try to lower dropout rates, but when rates exceed the national average, administrators panic and sometimes exert exceptional efforts to find and retain at-risk students. The United States Department of Education has repeatedly named Florida as a state displaying an unusually high percentage of dropouts. Consequently, for many years state authorities have grasped at various programs they hoped would reduce this rate, and they strongly encouraged local school districts to try new ideas. Florida's legislature cooperated with these efforts and passed their version of laws that prevent granting a driver's license to a dropout. Florida dropout-prevention programs have been feeble, but they always managed to keep some at-risk students in school. Continued attendance of these reluctant scholars usually meant that their classes had another undereducated pupil who probably wouldn't and couldn't change a pattern of many years. Their fellow students also suffered since they had to interact with peers who didn't want to be in school. Often these at-risk students were disruptive in classes to the dismay of their instructors. When this happened, it was nothing new because these pupils had been frustrating their teachers for years.

The school board in Indian River County in Florida confronted the problems that accompanied keeping at-risk students in regular classes, and they looked for a solution. A new use of computers was suggested: remove these students from regular classrooms, and let the machines teach them. Since instructors didn't relish the difficulties involved in trying to teach these students, it was an opportunity to try something new without arousing opposition from teachers.

After considering the options, the school board authorized the establishment of a program using computers. It was begun in Vero Beach High School in 1987. School authorities put the at-risk students into a separate section where teaching was done, not by teachers, but by computers. Teachers in these classes became facilitators of learning. Instructors in regular classes were relieved. Computerized education took students, who were not keeping up, out of their mainstream classes. Therefore, both instructors and other pupils in these classes benefited immediately.

After the Vero Beach experiment began, results were beyond expectations. One indication of its success is that many other school districts in Florida investigated and copied the program. Schools from across the nation also heard of its achievements and visited the school.

To become candidates for the program, students had to be behind academically and unable to graduate with their class. They also had to be seriously considering dropping out. After beginning the computer program, Vero Beach authorities checked to see if the program was accomplishing what was intended. Obviously it had one expected and desirable result: computers aided teachers of ordinary students by removing at-risk students from regular classes where they often misbehaved. Another meaningful gain appeared: authorities found they were exceeding their goals for retention of students. Previously they had been having difficulty in retaining 60 percent of at-risk students. With computer instruction, their retention rate skyrocketed, eventually to over 80 percent. Computers were obviously effective. They kept at-risk students attending school, more than any other type of dropout program ever tried in that district. Moreover, an unexpected revelation jolted pupils: school could be fun. Most of these perennially deficient students had never experienced this sensation.

When the school examined results beyond mere retention rates, the unthinkable appeared. Students in dropout-prevention programs taught by computers were going beyond mere physical presence. They were learning! They were absorbing knowledge better and faster than they had ever done before. Students, who had shown no inclination to retain knowledge or to want to progress, suddenly were being educated. A bizarre possibility electrified the students: they might even graduate. These were students who had never, in their recent memories, thought about this unlikely accomplishment. Overnight they decided it might be a good idea to try since this success now seemed within reach. With encouragement from their facilitating teachers, they calculated how a high school diploma would add sizable sums to their earning power for the rest of their lives. They were impressed. Now that graduation was, at least, a remote possibility, they decided it was worth belated efforts to get there.

These pupils had been dawdling along academically for years. Overcoming this handicap in the time remaining would require an instantaneous change. To graduate they had to make up, not lost months but vanished years. For a decade, they had been learning less than other students. They had a lot of catching up to do. Strangely and unexpectedly, this happened in the computer classrooms. Students, behind and about to drop out, suddenly began to retain in one year what ordinary students had taken several years to learn. Facilitating teachers in the programs reported another change in these at-risk students. Their long history of being disruptive and difficult students meant nothing. Although they had been the acknowledged bane of teachers throughout much of their academic careers, they now had a radically different attitude.

Judy Jones, the original coordinator for the computer program in Vero Beach, had transferred to the school that first year when the program began. The radical new classrooms with computers as teachers showed immediate external results. Other instructors who walked by her computer labs in that initial year were in open astonishment. They had tried to deal with these same students and knew their history of many years of misbehaving. When they saw them now earnestly working at their computers with little untoward behavior, they found it difficult to understand. When they discovered they were not only behaving but were also learning, their amazement burst forth in an accolade that new faculty members rarely receive. The other teachers named Judy Jones "Teacher of the Year" in her first year in the school.

Previously undisciplined students were showing discipline. Students, who had been unable to learn, were now being educated. The extent of the gains they made is a still more remarkable part of the story. It requires some background for those unfamiliar with education.

The GED Program

An examination has been used in America since 1942 called the Test of General Educational Development, commonly referred to by its initials, the GED. It was developed to enable pupils who had dropped out of school, but who had learned as much as ordinary high school graduates, to obtain the equivalent of a high school diploma. At its inception during World War II, many high school students had left school early to join the armed forces. Passing the GED test allowed bright service men and women to gain the status that accompanied high school graduation. Moreover, when they left the service after the war, they were able to enter college without returning to high school.

The GED program was an immense success and was kept after the war. The American Council on Education continues to sponsor it today. It is not, nor was it ever intended as an easy way to obtain a high school diploma. The test requires candidates to show they have "acquired a level of learning comparable to that of high school graduates,"[1] and is usually given to adults after their school days. States have discretionary leeway in deciding how high to make the passing grade. Florida has established for its students a passing score on the GED among the highest in the nation.[2] The national GED Testing Service has compiled data showing how graduating high school seniors across the country would do based on various score requirements. Under the Florida criteria, only 66 percent of regular graduates receiving normal high school diplomas across the United States can pass the test.[3]

Authorities in Vero Beach knew their pupils in computerized education were learning. Nonetheless, they were unable to graduate them because twenty-four credits were required. Credits depend primarily on time spent in completed classes. Even if the computer students knew enough, they still lacked sufficient credits. Therefore, authorities decided to use the GED exam as a replacement. This option set up a horrendous complication for the at-risk students trying to graduate. Only 66 percent of successful graduates can pass the GED with the Florida requirements after twelve normal years of learning in school. The at-risk students had been markedly behind when they entered the program. Now the school demanded that they not only equal other graduates but that they do better than one-third of them. If they failed, their quest of a diploma had also failed.

Odds against these students passing the GED were enormous. No one unfamiliar with the power of computers could have given them much chance to graduate. When the tests were given and scored, questions about the effectiveness of this novel way of teaching vanished. Computers had effectively overcome those oppressive negative odds. Eighty-five percent of students taught by computers pass the GED with the Florida requirements on their first attempt.

Other School Systems

Results from other school districts that followed Vero Beach are equally impressive. Broward County, with Ft. Lauderdale as its hub, claims to be "The Nation's Largest Fully Accredited School System." Authorities studied what had happened in Vero Beach and then established a similar computer program. The dropout program in this district was placed under the direction of Dale Kadlecek, Ed.D., Assistant Principal at Northeast High School. Dr. Kadlecek reported outcomes in a paper he delivered after a full year of computerized education.

In that first year eighty-one students were enrolled. At the conclusion of the year, 83 percent of the students had remained in school during the year. The goal had been to retain 60 percent. Even that goal had been too optimistic for previous dropout-prevention programs. An 83 percent retention rate would have made previous programs unqualified successes in this school district.[4] The program also produced learning results that agreed with the startling outcomes in Vero Beach. Broward followed the same policy and allowed students who were chronologically of an age to graduate to take the GED. Twenty-three students fit this classification. None of them had any chance of graduating, however, under the record they had compiled before entering the computer program. All were behind academically. After computer teaching, twenty-two out of twenty-three of these academically weak, at-risk students completed the GED test successfully! Again, youths who had been years behind were able in only one year to learn enough to pass an examination 34 percent of high school graduates across America would fail. Computerized education had made this seemingly impossible achievement a reality.

Broward's program added another twist that accentuated the value of computer learning. Students who entered the program before their senior year were ineligible to graduate that year. These pupils needed additional challenges. Dr. Kadlecek and his staff worked out an agreement with the local community college enabling students to attend while still in high school. They thereby accumulated college credits they could use after they had finished high school. Students, who were at-risk and about to drop out of high school, were suddenly college students. This result, by itself, ought to make every educator in the nation take notice.

The program has now spread to over twenty other districts in Florida. Outcomes continue to be excellent. Since the program has been duplicated throughout the state, these convincing results are not due solely to the exceptional ability of one teacher, Judy Jones, who headed the initial program.

Computers and Younger Students

Can computerized education also be effective with younger students? After their success in the high school program, authorities in Indian River County decided to try to stop potential dropouts at an earlier level. They began identifying students in the fourth or fifth grade who were developing patterns that made them likely dropouts later. As with the high school, these were usually students who were behind and uninterested. Pupils in grade schools are younger, and no one was sure they could adapt to computerized education in the same successful way as older students.

The results again were outstanding. Students, who had no interest in school and were failing consistently, suddenly began to learn. They not only learned; they enjoyed it. Sometimes, in one year, they accomplished what ordinary students took two or three years to do. Another result from this program mimics the outcome in the high school: children entering the program are behind most students academically; those leaving are often ahead of many ordinary students who avoided the at-risk category. The new program is similar to the one in the high school. Officials even brought students from the high school at-risk program to encourage the grade school students. Shortly before, the high school students themselves had been classified as at-risk students. Now they are counseling younger at-risk students.

What Happens in These Programs?

Computers teach the pupils. Despite a history of years of indifference or even hostility to schooling by these students, something changes. Computer programs are able to hold their interest, to challenge them, and to make learning interesting. Students are not isolated with a computer. Teachers continually encourage them. These instructors admit that when they first began the program, they expected to use computers extensively but also to continue their accustomed instructing. They soon found that any teaching computers were programmed to provide could be successfully delivered by the machines without additional instruction by them. Computers furnish lesson materials, and teachers act as coaches or facilitators. Each student moves at his or her own pace. Teachers encourage students, but computers teach.

These results are accomplished with software that is good by today's standards but is still woefully weak as contrasted with what could be developed. These classes are not "cram" courses where students are buried in academic endeavors for untold hours on end. Trying to enforce unpleasant learning with this type of student is self-defeating. Students spend only two to four hours per day in the computer labs. The universal atmosphere in classes is one of youths working diligently while having fun. Onlookers wouldn't suspect that these are pupils who had previously shown a negative attitude toward education. I have visited several different district programs. My reaction everywhere was the same: these are students who enjoy what they are doing. One company supplying software for these programs believes a student with two hours of computer lab instruction can equal what a student would accomplish in one month of regular classes. The instructor who first told me about this felt that this was an accurate appraisal. She made this judgement after two years of working in the computer program. Previously, she had had several years of teaching in regular classes.

Conclusion

These programs dramatize the efficacy of computerized education and show that computers, without a teacher between the children and the machines, can teach students of different ages, teach them well, and make learning enjoyable. That epitomizes the basic argument of this whole book. When schools fully embrace true computerized education, the dreadful state of much present schooling will change overnight. Almost every child will learn to read early. They will then be able to enjoy education, as they should.

Poor students will not be the only beneficiaries of computerized education; average and bright students will achieve equal, or even greater gains. Specific examination of how and why computerization can revolutionize schooling will begin in Chapter 9. Before then, however, it will be helpful to highlight more generic features of computers when properly applied in education. That will be the subject of the next chapter.

Chapter 6

Overview of Computers in Education

S ince the beginning of the industrial revolution, machines have been extending human power. Railroad engines inaugurated previously unimagined speed. For the first time, man was able to move faster than a horse. Railroads, however, have limits. They must follow rails that are permanently in place. Then came automobiles, not bound by rails and able to move independently. Nonetheless, they still had constraints; they had to move on the ground. Airplanes followed automobiles and enlarged those boundaries, but other restrictions remained. Railroads and cars and airplanes can't go beyond the broad category that may be termed transportation. Automobiles and airplanes, for example, don't manufacture goods or keep detailed records. Machines always had certain limited areas within which they could operate until computers arrived.

In their brief time, computers have driven, with blazing speed, radical alterations in innumerable areas and have left their effects almost everywhere. Without their guidance, the space program would cease and modern telephone networks would collapse. Scientific advances are dependent upon them. Businesses of every size have discovered their power and versatility and would now find it painfully difficult to operate as they did before these machines arrived. Financial markets grind to a crawl whenever their computers shut down temporarily. The list of beneficiaries of this modern technology is almost endless.

The only important field that computers have failed to change significantly is education. The United States has probably added as many computers proportionately to students as any nation in the world. Nonetheless, these millions of computers have had a minuscule effect on student learning. While technology brings modernization with blinding rapidity in many fields, education plods along as it has done for ages. The only major improvement that schools have universally embraced in the last two centuries has been the introduction of blackboards in the late nineteenth century. Serious changes in education have been minimal since then. As the Congressional Office of Technology Assessment complained:

> In general, classrooms today resemble their ancestors of 50 and 100 years ago much more closely than do today's assembly plants, scientific laboratories, and operating rooms. A number of information technologists point out that if business organizations today evolved at the same rate as the schools, they would still be using quill pens instead of electronic word processors.[1]

Although computers have been a powerful force in other industries, defenders of present practices would claim that greater reliance on computers in schooling is impossible because education is different. It deals with minds, not with mere facts and figures. That comment overlooks a fundamental aspect of the machines. Computers are successful with facts and figures because they are extensions of the human mind. Computers share the power of human intelligence because they are directed by, and are completely dependent upon, the directions that the minds of people can give them. Consequently, they have abolished many restrictions that bind other machines. Neither a mind nor a computer can carry people or materials, or cut metal or take photographs. Both can, however, direct other machines that perform these actions.

Computers have the ability to follow slavishly written or oral instructions, and this differentiates them from all other machines. It is their dominant attribute. These instructions are called programming or software. Each instruction for a computer is a simple statement that the machine can read and interpret. One programming instruction can be joined with hundreds or thousands of others. Together they provide awesome power. They can command computers to carry out actions and ideas that are complex and had not previously been contemplated outside the realm of pure human intelligence.

Playing chess is an example. Great minds have long been fascinated by chess, and masters of the game have been lauded for their brilliance. Computers are now sufficiently adept at playing that they can crush almost any opponent anywhere. As the machines advance further, computers will probably be able consistently to defeat anyone, even champion chess masters, if circumstances provide an incentive for human minds to write the intricate and essential instructions necessary. Without this human programming, computers are useless. With it, however, they emulate the minds that guide them but add two startling improvements: electronic speed and a massive memory. These additional attributes explain why computers can exceed the power of the minds behind them; why, for example, programmers can develop software that will defeat champion chess players although the programmers themselves are not champions.

Speed and memory combined with the human minds directing them, are the attributes that have enabled these machines to pervade and conquer the world with astonishing swiftness. Within these astounding extensions of human intelligence reside the keys needed to open the elusive revolution in education. Many dynamic benefits that flow from programming or software are particularly pertinent in education. I will here touch upon some of them.

General Benefits of Programming in Education

Flexibility

Human minds are eminently flexible, and computers, as their extensions, share that trait. Potential goals of programming are limitless, and the possible approaches to reaching any specific objective are extensive. This flexibility will allow software writers to lavish an abundance of learning opportunities on students. Pupils are not all alike. They differ in intelligence and interests and come from diverse backgrounds. Even an individual pupil may change from one day to the next depending on his or her emotional and physical conditions. Programming can overcome these variations. Diverse approaches can be used, not only with separate students but also with the same pupil at various times. As a child learns, the computer will continually evaluate his or her progress. The machine will review or repeat lessons as needed and will permit and encourage the learner to progress faster when the lesson has been mastered, or will slow the pace until the pupil grasps the material. It will diagnose errors and then provide remedial exercises before moving forward. It will also make lessons stimulating and interesting to enhance learning and retention. Moreover, software will be upgraded continually.

Education will never again remain stagnant. It will mutate from a static specialty, unchanged for centuries, to an evolving and advancing science.

Using established techniques of teachers

Programmers won't have to reinvent effective routines. They will be able to copy and use the skillful teaching techniques that minds of human instructors have developed over many ages. An example of computers imitating teachers is in analysis of errors. Experienced teachers often uncover a deficiency through incorrect answers that a student gives on a test or during a recitation. Whenever a critical error appears, a perceptive teacher understands that the student missed a fundamental point. By capitalizing on this background knowledge supplied by teachers, programmers can enable computers to identify the same difficulties. Although a computer cannot "understand," it can be programmed to recognize types of errors. Then it can also apply fitting remedies. Problems can be set up in the computer that will show when a specific student deficiency is present. The machines will generate and retain in their vast memories the correct answer and an extensive series of likely incorrect answers. The speed of the machine as it analyzes answers will enhance its effectiveness.

Misunderstanding of negative numbers can provide an example, and a simple problem will illustrate the principle:

$$+386$$
$$-(-125)$$
$$\overline{}$$
$$??????$$

The correct answer, of course, is 511. A common mistake might develop a solution of 261 or 136. Anyone confused by negative numbers might come to either erroneous solution. The computer would also find "261" and "136" in its memory. If either answer appeared as the student's response, the computer would again explain negative numbers and give a brief example or two. It would note that a fundamental error about negative numbers had occurred. Then it would provide more problems for the pupil. If a similar inaccuracy reappeared in another response, the machine would be aware of the previous difficulty and immediately provide further and more basic assistance. Additional help would continue until the student showed sufficient understanding.

This salutary technique flows from its use of teachers' experiences of the way children sometimes confuse negative numbers. Analysis of errors will be only one of many instances where the accumulated wisdom of teachers will aid programmers, just as the accumulated wisdom of earlier instructors has always helped new teachers. Software writers will bolster programs with ideas used for centuries. Almost all known techniques will be used by computers as educational programming matures.

For example, on a discussion of causes of the First World War, those who have taught the subject understand difficulties that students have when they try to sort out the conditions that led to the conflict. Teachers, from their training and experience, can show programmers how to emphasize frequently overlooked or misunderstood issues and to make students aware of happenings, both deliberate and unplanned. Instructors can help programmers impress on students the vast panoply of causes and pseudo-causes that are involved in major cataclysms, using that war or any other conflict as an example. These teachers can also point out to programmers how they are able to make history come alive for students by stressing the personalities or strategy involved. Software writers can use this accumulated expertise to provide instructive material that will make learning lasting and more enjoyable. When these tested deliveries have been programmed into the computer, they will be used whenever they will help educate a student. Software will enable the computer itself to determine when they are appropriate.

Improvements will continue by engaging other astute humans whose brilliance will be extended through computers. The combination of educators, other experts, and programmers combining their immense talents while taking advantage of the resources of computers will result in a continual flow of teaching enhancements.

Going beyond teachers' ordinary skills.

While computers imitate and take ideas from the vast store of knowledge acquired over many ages, their speed and memory will propel them beyond the natural limitations of people. The machines can track multitudes of happenings that would be beyond human abilities. For example, computers can count and remember how often a specific mistake is made by an individual student and by thousands of students, and then can notify programmers that a specific error or genre of error is being made frequently by the learners. With this information, writers of software will be able to redesign the portion of the program dealing with that confusion. They will employ a different or expanded method of instruction to lessen the likelihood that the mistake will continue to occur. Programmers will again be informed by feedback if the student perplexity is repeated.

Software provides additional ancillary advantages. For example, when an outstanding teacher develops a new method to improve student performance, usually only the classes of that teacher benefit. When computer programmers working with knowledgeable educators develop a better and enriching approach, they will make it available to every student using that software, wherever the machines are located.

An additional benefit will follow. A student, because of his or her unique weaknesses, may find a specific teacher's method difficult even if that teacher is excellent at instructing other students. Software allows the machine to use different techniques to reach diverse pupils. Every computer through its programming can mimic more than one model teacher. It can use whichever style is effective depending on needs of students. I will return to this important characteristic when I cite the value of individualized instruction.

Enhancing other teaching aids

Another important educational improvement that the wonders of programming will introduce flows from the capacity of computers to control and totally integrate audiovisual presentations into the instruction of each student. In computerized education, these can be viewed on the monitors by students, and software will control them completely. Audiovisual displays are called multimedia in computer terminology. More than the name has changed; the whole concept is vastly expanded. A full chapter later in this book is necessary merely to hint at the dazzling possibilities of multimedia controlled by computers and their software.

Comparing lessons stored in the machines' memories with those found in textbooks illustrates another area where programming can improve on current teaching aids. When books are printed each copy must be identical with every other one produced at that time. Lack of absolute uniformity, however, could have advantages. For example, history might be better remembered if happenings in different geographical locations were highlighted for the pupils living in those areas. Computer programs can provide valuable variations, and they won't be limited only to past happenings. When scientific breakthroughs occur, updated material can be added at once over telephone lines to all copies wherever they are used. It will even be possible for sectarian schools to have certain concepts, which they wish to stress, easily added or inserted into the software for use in their schools. Specific school districts may want some ideas to receive more attention. Software writers will be able to accommodate their wishes, often with only minimal added cost. Obviously, this may pose philosophical problems that I cannot solve here. My only objective is to point out what can be done.

The world confronts a frightening predicament. Education needs improvement that will allow the work force to survive in a highly technological society. Nonetheless, schools misuse the most powerful and effective tool of change in history. This blatant waste would be horrible at any point in history. With the current requirements in education, squandering this available remedy is a catastrophe. For computers to accomplish in education what they have done elsewhere, one new element is essential: they must be allowed to teach students without a human in the intermediary position between the child and the computer. This failure to allow computers to teach is the reason technology thus far has been a dismal failure in schools. I will examine this phenomenon in the next two chapters.

Computers have taken a major position in the world because they are able to execute many tasks more effectively than humans can. In education, they are able to communicate information more efficiently, and they can do it with panache. They can fascinate while they teach.

When I use the term "computers," I mean more than the basic machine. I include multimedia capability, present and emerging, which computers can integrate and direct, and ancillary technology connected with them, especially communications through modems. For simplicity, the contemplated full use of computers will be termed "computerized education" throughout this book.

Basic Objections To Computerized Education

In recent years, several new technologies have been developed that were touted by their adherents as able to revitalize education. Teaching machines, audiovisual presentations, movies, filmstrips, and videos were hailed as potential saviors that would bring a dynamic transformation of schools. Education withstood each of these intrusions and emerged virtually unchanged. The reaction to claims that any new technology can bring a major revision will be greeted with amused disbelief and quickly dismissed by some authorities. They've heard this trite assertion of super powers before about these other novelties, and nothing happened. Why expect this latest gimmick to upset a system that has shown itself to be inflexible for a century?

This time, however, we are dealing with instruments whose range and power are unprecedented. Their unique qualities have enabled them to remake countless other fields. No previous invention has forced similar adjustments. Computers can achieve in education what they have done elsewhere. They can bring a total turnabout. Merely because other educational modifications have been unduly praised and have failed is an ineffectual argument to prove that no invention can ever revolutionize schools. I ask readers to evaluate the characteristics that computers bring before dismissing them.

Even acknowledgment of the power and unique characteristics of these machines does not ensure their immediate acceptance. Arguments against assigning to computers one of life's most vital components, education, are manifold. The most obvious objection is contained in this question: "How could a machine do what Miss Smith did for me in the fourth grade?" Many other legitimate hesitations exist:

- Machines will break down, and students will be left with nothing to do.
- Computer programs always have bugs, and again, the students will be left without material.
- Computers can teach only certain facts, not the more important higher-order thinking.
- Some students will deliberately manhandle computers and destroy them.

- Computers can be dangerous to the eyesight of students because of the need to read from the screen.
- Computers can be dangerous because of Carpal Tunnel Syndrome, a malady that pains thousands of people in offices where computers are used regularly.
- The cost of giving every student a computer is prohibitive.
- A machine cannot make judgments that a human can make.
- A machine cannot teach values.
- A machine cannot develop interaction among students.
- A machine cannot give necessary and meaningful personal attention to students.
- Pupils will waste time if no teacher checks on them.
- Bright students will discover how to use computers to alter and destroy the system.
- One student will be able to take the test of another student since no human will be checking.
- A school system with computers as teachers will turn out automatons, not warm, friendly humans.
- Some students will be unable to use computers either through fright or incompetence and will receive no education.
- If computers could be teachers, schools would currently use them in that way since they already possess millions of the machines.

Some of these objections are valid and some are merely specious. All must be addressed. Answers to these difficulties will be brought out as we move along. Responses will be summarized in the final chapter. If any reader might be tempted to move there from this point, I must say "Whoa! Don't jump to the last chapter now! That's permissible when you are reading mystery stories but forbidden in books on education. We'll get there, but some groundwork must be in place."

WHY
COMPUTERS
ARE
INEFFECTIVE
TODAY

Chapter 7

Problems Confronting Teachers

*A*fter the previous exposition of the generic advantages of computers in education but before an analysis of the specific gains they will bring, an answer to an obvious question is required. "If computers are so sensational, why haven't they brought any notable improvement to education until now?"

One simple reason why the machines have not bettered education appreciably is immediately apparent. Hundreds of thousands of instructors don't use computers in their classes and couldn't use them if they wanted to. They don't know how.[1] The immediate result of this lack of training of teachers is that computer equipment in schools today is mostly unused, perhaps an hour or two per student per week.[2]

This lack of proficiency is true not only for instructors who were in classrooms before computers became common in schools but also applies to new teachers just starting their careers. The American Association of Colleges for Teacher Education surveyed ninety schools of education. They found that "the faculty rated only 58 percent of the students as prepared to teach with computers." Apparently even that discouraging figure had been optimistically inflated by the professors because researchers also found that "only 29 percent of the education students felt ready to teach with computers."[3] This predicament of newcomers is the necessary result of their training. The education school professors are themselves unskilled and untrained in the art of using computers in teaching. The Congressional Office of Technology commented on the "lack of expertise of many education school faculty."[4]

If the present lack of training of teachers were not a sufficient obstacle to successful use of computers in today's schools, a more difficult hurdle can also be recognized: initial teacher training is not sufficient. The Congressional Office of Technology summed up the predicament when it said, "Teachers need continuing training as the technology changes, as new and more effective applications are developed, and as more is learned about learning with technology."[5] Preparing teachers to use computers is a process that can never be completed.

If, however, computerized education were implemented, in which the machines were used to teach without an intermediary instructor, the need for constant training and retraining of teachers would be eliminated. Teachers need and want continuing education, but it is more valuable if it is given either in their area of expertise or in methods of helping students, not in how to try to use computers.

The lack of training is one reason why only a small percentage of the teachers in the nation use computers in their classes. The Congressional Office also pointed out others that apply even to those instructors who are knowledgeable about technology when it said:

> Teachers who have taught with computers agree that— at least initially—most uses of computers make teaching more challenging. Individualizing lessons, matching software to curriculum, scheduling student computer time, monitoring use, providing assistance, and trouble shooting - all add burdens to the teacher's time.... The net effect is increased demand on teachers' time and creativity.... very few teachers have adequate time for planning and preparing to use technology.[6]

After examination of each challenge separately, a pattern develops showing clearly the frustrations that fall on teachers when they use computers. Simultaneously, we can see that these difficulties would vanish if computers were used without teachers as intermediaries.

"individualizing lessons" Even the best teacher finds it a monstrous difficulty to individualize lessons for each student in any classroom. Students are at different learning levels, and dedicated teachers struggle continually to surmount this immense obstacle. When computers are used in today's classrooms, problems are intensified because another level, the computer, exists between teacher and individual student. Theoretically, when using computers, teachers might assign different students to different parts of lessons depending on the progress of pupils. That, however, would require that the teacher be able to analyze accurately the condition of the learning of thirty students on that particular day and know the intricacies of the computer lessons with uncanny thoroughness. Even if teachers had these super skills, computer programs intended for only one class would lack many instructional steps demanded by the unique requirements of individual students. If teachers had different programs available, they still could not decide exactly what level of computer instruction was optimum for each student. Computers, if they were unhindered, could easily analyze and determine individual student needs and provide appropriate lessons. The teacher's attempt to individualize instruction provides a monumental burden for teachers without the gains that computers can provide.

"**matching software to curriculum**" Teachers must choose a software program that they have decided will help them and supplement their instruction while keeping their curriculum requirements always in the forefront. Programmers can create software that will satisfy the needs of the total curriculum but only if computers are responsible for the complete education of students. If computers were instructing without a teacher, they would not be bound by predetermined limits of a software package intended for only one class. If a machine discovered that a student was missing information or skills that should have been learned four years earlier, it would return to that level. When it found a student ready to go to the next level, it would immediately provide the advanced material. It would integrate learning to a degree impossible today when computers are used only to augment the instruction of a teacher. Again, teachers waste their valuable resources trying to match software to curriculum because software writers can do it more easily and more efficiently. There will be more about this in the next chapter.

"**scheduling student computer time**" The same principle applies here. Teachers must try to accomplish what would be automatic if computers were responsible for teaching. If students had full access to a machine as they would in computerized education, scheduling problems would vanish. Providing an individual computer for every student in present classes is impractical. Most teachers will not use them, and the others will employ them only for brief periods.

"monitoring use" Teachers must try to supervise how thirty pupils use their individual computers. Every teacher, who has thirty eyes operating independently of each other, finds this task is easy. For those who have only two eyes and can focus on only one object at a time, it is more difficult—*impossible* may be a more apt term. Computers are better able to oversee their use by individual pupils than is a teacher. Software writers could build monitoring into lessons. As a simple example, they could program machines to query students when a certain length of time had elapsed without interaction from the student. The machine would immediately set about solving the difficulty, whatever it might be. It could take appropriate remedial action if frivolous interactions took place. If necessary, programming could alert authorities. Each machine would be responsible for one student instead of one teacher trying to watch and supervise thirty students.

"providing assistance and trouble shooting" This obstacle pertains primarily to technical problems stemming from computers. A few teachers become adept at computer usage. Most do not. People who use computers regularly are often ill-equipped for trouble shooting. This help could be provided by the computer if it had been incorporated into the original programming. In complete computerized education, programmers will arrange for automatic feedback to them of problems, and they will then make changes in programs to decrease constantly the difficulties students encounter. If more help is needed, students will be able to reach outside experts at any time. I will discuss this option in Chapter 21. Teachers are not prepared for the job of trying to be computer experts or technical wizards. Placing them in that position is inefficient, wastes their valuable time, and gives them another useless burden

All these daunting problems now confront teachers when they try to use computers in their classrooms. Teachers are already grossly overburdened. Recall the end of the above citation from the Congressional Office: "very few teachers have adequate time for planning and preparing to use technology." With these problems confronting teachers when they use computers, their attitudes are, understandably, often tepid and sometimes antagonistic toward the machines. Present use of computers burdens teachers and provides minimal help for education.

The basic difficulties of teachers when trying to integrate computers into their classrooms help explain why computers have accomplished little in schools. Unfortunately, this is only a part of the difficulty. Even if by some miracle all teachers were suddenly made computer literate and were all filled with a desire to use computers, there would remain other and more potent obstacles, which relate to the creation of necessary software. That is the subject of the next chapter.

Chapter 8

Problems Confronting Programmers

*I*n the short history of computers, software producers have been remarkable in developing successful programs for banking, communications, management, medicine, finance, space, accounting, publishing, manufacturing, research—the list is almost endless. One giant exception stands out: education. According to the Congressional Office of Technology Assessment "there is a general consensus that most software does not yet sufficiently exploit the capacity of the computer to enhance teaching and learning."[1]

Software producers have been able to revolutionize other industries, yet have failed in education. Why?

An obvious and preliminary question first needs an answer: "Have they tried hard enough?" They should have, if only because the number of potential customers ought to activate their profit-making juices. Every student could use many programs. Forty million potential customers are waiting in the United States alone, hundreds of millions more in other nations. Without question, software companies got the message about the huge market. They have made massive efforts. When the Congressional Office issued the above complaint about weak software, over nine hundred companies had already developed over ten thousand educational programs in the United States. Additions have continued unabated since then.

Lack of outstanding software, therefore, is not due to half-hearted attempts by companies. Something is different in education that hinders development of superior programs. These mediocre results are due to the way that schools employ computers today. The present procedures make it virtually impossible for programmers to develop and sell distinguished software to schools and for schools to use software of the highest caliber. The underlying reasons can be arranged under three basic groupings:

1. Teacher variations
2. An inherently fragmented market
3. Time and curriculum requirements

Teacher Variations

Computer software doesn't have the responsibility for educating pupils. Teachers have that obligation. They decide how it should be done, and they must choose software to help them carry out their ideas of instructing. Software developers can't start with the sole objective of writing programs that will teach children as well as is possible for a computer to instruct. The primary goal of programmers must be to assist teachers to teach children as well as is possible for those teachers to instruct. Although in theory these two goals are the same, there are profound differences.

The individual teacher's method must remain the predominant element in every classroom. Programmers developing educational software must create programs that will aid instructors and appeal to those instructors. Obviously, teachers have unique talents. Their differences are pronounced, and education has always allowed for these variations—even encouraged them. Although standards for classes have been established, each teacher necessarily has considerable leeway in conveying the required material to students. The instructor's choice is not based on an arbitrary whim. It depends on his or her skill, knowledge, energy, and training. Each teacher has a unique combination of natural traits and acquired background. Teachers have many valid reasons to avoid using computers as the last chapter brought out. If, however, they decide to employ the machines, all their individual characteristics influence them as they consider how they want to prepare students before they use computers, how much to permit computers to cover, where to place computer instruction into their teaching plan, how to integrate computers with their testing and grading, and how much time to give students to interact with computer lessons.

The absolute quality of the software cannot predominate in buying decisions by teachers. They must select a program that is compatible with their style of teaching. Otherwise, they and the computers will be out of harmony. Even when many teachers wish to use computers to teach the same subject, each may prefer different software because of his or her unique skills and training. This need to accommodate programs to individual traits of instructors creates an immense hurdle for software publishers. Millions of teachers mean multitudes of preferences and goals. This overriding obligation to accord with the personal and diverse requirements of teachers is basic to the inability of programmers to develop educational software for schools that will take full advantage of the power of computers.

An Inherently Fragmented Market

A pragmatic obstacle also hinders software writers: realizing a profit by developing software is made more difficult because diverse teacher wishes and needs result in a smaller market for any one program. This hindrance is less damaging than teacher variations but flows from them and warrants mention here. Programming is costly, and companies engaged in development need to make money. Despite the huge numbers of students, teacher variations limit potential customers for any one program. The result is less impetus for companies to expend substantial amounts of time and money developing software. Interestingly, Microsoft, which is the foremost software producer in the world, has failed to make a significant entrance into the potentially mammoth school market.

The Congressional Office suggested a solution to the problem of costs. They proposed that the government take part in developing software.[2] This federal involvement might allow programs to be written without regard to how well the programs would sell. Although the idea has some merit, under present conditions this policy would be costly without ensuring an improvement in education. Teachers would still use only the software that fits with their needs even if it were free. The core problem of divergences among teachers would remain, and even the federal government could not expend sufficient money to cover all variables among teachers.

In recent years, software producers have been trying to overcome the financial handicap of this diverse market by directing their sales pitches to school boards and superintendents. These authorities can choose programs for the entire system and can buy many copies and impose them on groups of teachers. Software companies avidly embrace this plan of marketing because it allows them to sell larger quantities of the same program. Teachers, however, don't like it. Where they do not select software but find it specified by school authorities, they have a history of overt or covert rebellion. Their hesitation is understandable because their many natural variations rule out the possibility that one computer program can serve them all well. When software is imposed upon them, instructors would have to alter their methods to achieve optimum results.

Teachers can't make these changes. They are not being obstinate. They can't revise drastically their methods unless they can do the impossible: change their individual talents, training, experience, and energy levels. At times, teachers ignore computer programs that are imposed by higher authorities almost completely. Sometimes they merely go through the motions of employing computers. I must repeat that teachers cannot be blamed for this impasse. Simultaneously, programmers are not at fault because they can't create one software program that will conform to innumerable different teaching methods and styles, and that will still be exceptionally effective when used in classrooms with students who also have different abilities and needs.

The multiple and major differences among teachers explain a portion of the inability of companies to develop remarkable programming. Hesitation of software companies to expend the large sums necessary to develop products that will be used only by a few teachers adds another hurdle. These, however, are only part of the problem. Other serious obstacles also challenge makers of software.

Time and Curriculum

Two substantial restraints that always bedevil teachers hinder software development: the hours available to teachers are limited, and the requirements of the curriculum they must follow are rigid. Teachers who use computers must finish their lessons in the periods allotted, and instructors regularly find they could use additional hours. The time they give students to interact with the machines must be taken from their block of available hours. Theoretically, computers should help them complete their teaching in less time.

This savings apparently doesn't help them appreciably as is shown by the little time that computer-using students spend on the machines.[3] Programmers, therefore, must incorporate their assistance into whatever time teachers can spare to use computers.

The ever present and important curriculum requirements are another obstacle. Teachers are responsible for covering a specified amount of material in their classes. Basic student weaknesses affect learning in many ways, but teachers are unable to address all individual needs and still cover the assigned material. An instructor attempting to teach ninth grade literature must focus primarily on covering the authors required for that class, not on improving basic sixth grade reading skills. Some students, however, would profit more from literature if they could read better. Writers can produce programs that will ferret out student needs and provide fitting antidotes for almost all student shortcomings. Remedying defects that are normally addressed in other classes, however, is not the reason that teachers choose their products. Programmers must, therefore, concentrate on producing software that will agree fully with the primary consideration of teachers: covering the assigned part of the curriculum. As a consequence, they must leave unattended the more basic needs of certain students.

Review and Confirmation

This chapter began by asking why companies producing software for education have been unable to duplicate their successes in other fields. The answer is that programmers cannot aim primarily to teach children but must try to help teachers with varied skills teach children, and their programming must simultaneously meet the time and curriculum requirements placed on teachers. The struggle is hopeless, and consequently, the world's producers of programming have created little exceptional educational software. The ultimate result is that the almost unlimited power of computers has had a negligible impact in education.

I can offer additional substantiation that these conclusions are correct. This evidence is derived from an occurrence that seems incredible at first sight but is understandable with the reasoning of this chapter: teachers do not regularly use the best software that programmers have created. The Congressional

Office of Technology decried a fundamental predicament: products that are highly rated by "Experts" because they represent the most innovative uses are not necessarily the ones preferred by most teachers.[4]

Teachers are a dedicated group. Although they bypass the best programs, they do not deliberately wish to shortchange students. They choose inferior software simply because of the necessary criterion for any selection: the programming must agree with each instructor's teaching agenda, individual talents, and specific time and curriculum requirements. No one program, even if it is objectively outstanding, can match the needs of many teachers because their requirements vary widely. Therefore, only a small percentage of instructors will find any particular program, however good it may be, suited to their individual needs.

The Answer

Present use of computers by teachers sharply limits the potential of computers but does not greatly enhance the capabilities of teachers nor make their jobs less difficult. Under the present system, the awesome teaching power of computers can never be fully used, and teachers can never be relieved of the time-consuming tasks that interfere with their true abilities to educate children. The solution is simple: free teachers from their usual duties, and let computers teach students without an intermediary human instructor.

If the primary goal of programmers were to provide the best education for students without worrying whether the programs conform to the different styles of teachers and their particular time and class curriculum restraints, these writers could develop software that would enable computers to teach every student effectively. They could build on the unsurpassed ability of the machines to provide individual instruction.

Why haven't schools taken what seems a logical step and allowed computers to teach? A major difficulty is the need to change established patterns, but another may be because teachers fear that this use of computers will denigrate their position in education. Their anxiety is unfounded. Computerized education will not harm teachers. Quite the contrary! Their results will improve. Their status will be boosted. The poor morale that riddles their ranks today will be bettered. They will be relieved of the boring and frustrating tasks that consume huge portions of their educational hours. They will devote more of their limited time to their primary passion: educating youth. They will be able to use their talents and dedication in more productive manners. I will show the gains that will accrue to teachers in Chapters 18, 19 and 20.

It is now appropriate to examine in depth the advantages that will come to education when computers in schools can duplicate their successes elsewhere.

SECTION IV

SPECIFIC
COMPUTER
ADVANTAGES

Chapter 9

Tutoring Individuals

Alexander the Great benefited by having a king, Philip of Macedon, as his father. The king was astute and had the power and foresight to recruit the brightest person in the known world, Aristotle, as the private tutor for his son. Not everyone can have a king for a father, but each student today can have a private tutor with even more knowledge than Aristotle. This tutor is a computer. Of all the advantages that computers will deliver to education, the foremost will be their capacity to act as individual tutors.

An ideal tutor can provide exceptional advantages for learning. Let us suppose that each of us could choose a perfect mentor for our child. We would select one who was knowledgeable in all subjects and who could tailor courses to the child's individual needs and abilities. We would want a tutor who would be aware of precisely what the child knew to prevent undue repetition, while ensuring that all necessary instruction was provided. We would pick one with enough time to give the pupil individual attention whenever needed without holding up other students. We would require this idealized teacher to have the flexibility to instruct a little differently sometimes when the child forgot something or had difficulty in grasping a point. Our child, of course, would never fall behind because of sickness or absence. The private tutor would always start the next class exactly where the previous one had ended.

We would want an additional virtue in our ideal tutor: an encouraging attitude. A story told by President John Kennedy illustrates how his father used this trait to help him to develop his self-confidence. Kennedy spoke about his father shortly after the first of his famous TV debates with Richard Nixon. He said that if he had walked out on the stage that night and had stumbled and fallen flat on his face before forty million viewers, his father's only comment would have been, "The way you picked yourself up off the floor was spectacular!"

President Kennedy's thought about his father may have been idealized. Nonetheless, it strikes a resonant note. We recognize that psychologically, it aids our development when we work with someone eager to praise, hesitant to find fault. Unfortunately, avoiding criticism is often difficult. A tone of voice or body language may sometimes unconsciously betray feelings. When a teacher finds that a student has forgotten something that has been repeated many times, reacting slightly and almost imperceptibly is an understandable human response. Somehow the pupil often interprets this correctly to mean, "You must remember. We've been over that again and again and again!"

Our model private tutor would never chastise the student when he or she was less than perfect including the inevitable occasions when an embarrassing stumble had occurred. Our hypothetical paragon, while pointing out mistakes, would be forever congratulating the child on its accomplishments and encouraging him or her to proceed further.

All these powerful characteristics we would choose for our child's private tutor are those that make a non-critical and eminently patient computer, endowed with almost unlimited knowledge, the ideal instructor. This teaching marvel can repeat and review a lesson as often as necessary and never betray the slightest feeling of exasperation, while simultaneously praising each forward step. Above all, the computer tutor can adapt to the needs of each student instead of requiring individuals to fit into a mold based on the average capabilities of many students.

Teaching to differing levels of ability, background, and interests has posed an eternal dilemma to educators. Teachers with a classroom of children know it is impractical to try to tailor lessons to each student. Personal attention, however, would be immensely helpful. Some students require additional explanations, while others have grasped the material and are ready to go on. Since having forty million private instructors is impossible, compromises are necessary, and teaching usually progresses at the average level of the class. Poorer students are left hanging in their confusion, and the brightest miss exciting challenges. With computers as tutors, the learning of one individual will never be hindered by the abilities or weaknesses of others. Each student will move at his or her own pace, unaffected by the rate of learning of any other student.

Theoretically, any student can ask questions in today's classes. In reality, students who are confused may not know enough to make an inquiry. Even when pupils know they need help, they are often embarrassed and don't wish to reveal their ignorance. Often only the most intelligent students dare to ask questions because they know that if they don't understand, neither does anybody else.

With individualized computer instruction, students will always be able to request help if something is unclear. They will be able to continue to show their lack of understanding until the problem is resolved without fear of appearing dumb before their peers. After the request for help, the computer will help pinpoint where the flaw lies. Then it will explain again the precise part of the lesson that bears on the student's weakness. Sometimes the computer might find a different explanation in its memory and present the material to the student in another way. The machines can always go back as far as necessary to ensure the student has a solid foundation on which to build.

When students are unaware of their poor learning or may not know the questions to ask, the computer itself will recognize their weakness through its constant evaluations and assessments. Whenever a pupil has not grasped a major point the computer will automatically review or repeat whatever is necessary. No student will feel disgraced or even embarrassed. Other pupils will be unaware of who requires more attention at a particular level, or when a hurdle is slowing a fellow learner.

Lack of intelligence may be the reason a student is unable to grasp material when it is first presented, but a host of other causes are also possible: previous learning, background, physical condition or simply a personality conflict with the teacher. The results, however, are the same: whenever a student fails to learn new material, he or she falls behind.

Difficulties compound afterward for the individual but also for teachers who have the student in subsequent grades. In today's classes, an individual student who falls behind usually stays behind. This inability to catch up is the crux of the dilemma of students, after years in schools, knowing little when they leave. They falter early, and additional classes only add to their confusion. They never have another opportunity to get the essential foundation they missed. Pupils who are deficient in basic mathematics are helpless trying to understand advanced math; those who don't know grammar will benefit little from a class in composition; students who cannot read are hopeless in virtually every worthwhile class.

With computers as tutors, no student will be overwhelmed because he or she is missing fundamentals. The computer will repeat material until each lesson has been sufficiently mastered. Only then will it move forward. Since today's computers have speech synthesis capability, they can start any place, even at the educational beginning, and teach pupils to read at the pace that is appropriate for each individual.

Computers will assist even before a course commences. They can test and evaluate the underlying knowledge of each student before the first lesson. For example, at the beginning of calculus, pupils can be tested on knowledge and understanding of the basic math and algebra necessary to master the subject. If anyone has a deficiency, the computer will provide a remedial lesson or course for that individual. The review can be given for as short or as extended a period as is necessary to bring the student up to standard. Lengthy reviews will be needed primarily at the onset of computerized education since later, the machines will ensure that pupils have mastered the prerequisites before they enter a new class. They might, however, need brushing up on material forgotten since the previous course was completed. The computer can easily provide help. A student will never be shoved into a hopeless struggle trying to learn without the needed foundation nor hold back other students who are ready to progress. The computer will not demand perfection, but it will require that the fundamentals necessary for the course be present before continuing.

As beneficial as individualized instruction will be for the poorer and average students, it will often be even more valuable for the brighter students. These have unique capabilities, and special attention and challenges often help them reach their intellectual limits. These students will be discussed further in Chapter 11.

All students, whether breathtakingly brilliant or woefully dull, or anywhere between these extremes, will benefit from individualized instruction. The immense power and versatility of computers as tutors will aid and simplify all learning for all students in all classes.

While individualized teaching represents the foremost advantage of computerized education, it is also the foundation for many other enhancements of learning that will follow when computers are allowed to operate unhindered. The next eight chapters will detail added benefits.

Chapter 10
Educating the Disadvantaged

A frightening aspect of the current crisis in education is that it has generated only a modicum of anxiety, and very little is being done about what is arguably the worst part: the twenty-five million adults whose lives are virtually destroyed by their illiteracy. Strange as it seems in a country that has made many of its greatest advances in the face of adversity, this crisis is worsening. With apologies to Browning, it may be apt to paraphrase him to describe the outlook for the nation's educational system today. "Grow sick along with me. The worst is yet to be." That appalling certainty stems from population predictions. The census bureau now estimates that the population of the United States will rise to 383 million by 2050, a 50 percent increase in less than sixty years. Today a little more than 20 percent of the population is from African-American or Hispanic backgrounds. In 2050 over 40 percent of the population will come from these same groups. These are the cultures undergoing the worst deprivation in current schools. Unless truly revolutionary action is taken, the nation will look back longingly to the days in the late 1990s when only twenty-five million illiterates lived in America.

Since everyone must go to school, it appears that anyone in America can have an education. This assumption is not true. Millions of children come from disadvantaged living environments. They grow up in families where adults can't read well, where books are scarce or non-existent, and where an appreciation of education is lacking. Naturally, these children grow up without any true regard for scholarship.

These intellectually impoverished youths attend the same schools as other children. Nonetheless, their chance to gain an education and to develop their own desire for academic learning is greatly diminished because of how they were raised. These children are classified, and in effect, branded, as "slow" students from the beginning of their educational experiences. They are behind the day they enter school, and few ever manage the excruciating feat of catching up. Most of them remain always behind with ever diminishing self-esteem. In turn, their pitiful schooling ensures that the cycle will continue in the next generation. Although Head Start programs can help to alleviate this problem and need to be expanded, the basic impediment remains.

These slow students begin with handicaps they didn't cause. When they attend school, additional obstacles, also beyond their control, may arise that intensify their difficult position. These impediments could include preconceived but camouflaged ideas of authorities or teachers. Few educators today would dare admit publicly to a belief that certain students are genetically inferior, but Lewis Terman, a leading psychologist and designer of I.Q. tests in the early twentieth century, was less hesitant. He said of immigrants, "Their dullness seems to be racial.... Children of this group should be segregated in special classes."[1] Terman was basing his judgment on what he had seen. Some educators today may base their judgments on what they perceive. When they observe that more of the slower students in schools come from certain races or cultures, their conclusions on inferiority may be similar, if unspoken, to those of Terman who saw poorer students coming from immigrant families. If so, add another obstacle for children from disadvantaged homes.

Realistically, even if administrators were completely impartial, slower students exceed the capabilities of schools today. Since classes must proceed at a pace that is faster than some students can grasp, these poorer students fall further and further behind. They are passed on to the next grade because some research indicates that holding students back is harmful to them. They enter a new grade without mastering the lessons of the previous one. The gap widens. Hope of catching up vanishes. Worse still, they quickly begin to feel that they cannot learn, and their fellow students feel the same about them because they are always behind.

Tracking

These students who are confronted by many innate hindrances often face yet another. They get caught up in a practice that is widespread throughout school systems called "tracking" where students are grouped by perceived ability. Instructors strongly and vigorously defend this pattern because it is much easier and, perhaps in some ways, more effective, to teach students who are in tracks. Groups with widely diverse abilities present multiple hindrances not present when students have more equal talents.

One supposed benefit of tracking is that students in lower tracks avoid classes where they will be compared with better students. Theoretically this avoids damage to their self-perception. Reality is different. Slower students and brighter students are fully aware of discrepancies between tracked classes, between "dumb" kids and "smart" kids. The conclusion of everybody must be the same: the "dumb" kids are inferior. The contention that tracking is an aid to developing or protecting the self-esteem of bottom-track students is patent nonsense.

Moreover, some teachers also look with disdain on students in these lower tracks, and they are not alone with their opinions. Even at the highest level, evidence of disparagement is available. Thomas Toch, who has studied and written extensively about education, quotes from school catalogs that denigrate these students by devastating descriptions: "English 284-285: for sophomores who are very slow learners and poor readers" and "English 283: for sophomores of below average ability."[2] As a consequence of the opinions of authorities, the education of slower students is different from, and inferior to, that of students in other tracks. In tracked classes today, both the caliber of courses and the quality of teachers are manifestly inferior for poorer students. These conditions are understandable. Since these students are already the weakest academically, it doesn't seem prudent or cost effective to administrators to burden them with material that they apparently can't absorb. Therefore schools provide less challenging classes for these pupils. Moreover, schools carry this reduction of standards to its logical conclusion and give them truly insipid subject matter. Poorer teachers can also be expected because instructing slower students provides less personal satisfaction. Consequently teachers who have a choice will usually opt for classes with brighter pupils. Substitutes or teachers who are only marginally qualified are often forced into classes of slower students.

Pupils in bottom tracks enter a situation where little is expected of them. Then in a form of self-fulfilling prophecy, these students are given pathetic and inadequate education. Writing by influential authors in recent years pointing out the evils of tracking has proliferated.[3] The National Governors Association took a position opposing it in its national education goals. A Carnegie Foundation task force voiced the same opposition in 1988.[4] Despite this powerful opposition, the system remains virtually intact in most school districts.[5] Tracking has had widespread use in schools for at least sixty years. The chances of eliminating the procedure under the present educational system are slim.

For the sake of argument, however, imagine that the teachers who support tracking suddenly allowed the system to vanish. What then? Opponents seem to suggest that if tracking were ended, poor education of slower students would also be eliminated. This contention is simply false. The problems are much deeper. Railing against the acknowledged disorder of tracking is like residents of Pompeii complaining about the noise of the rumblings of Vesuvius. Neither the noise nor tracking is the critical destructive force. Eliminating tracking would leave the underlying tragedy in place.

Current Deficiencies

At present, no way out of the miasma exists for these disadvantaged students. Obviously, mere attendance does not ensure learning. One potential and seemingly simple solution has caught the fancy of politicians on all sides of the ideological spectrum: end social promotion. This widespread approval of the nation's leaders might indicate that the idea has merit. In reality, the emphasis on this supposed answer is another example of seeking a quick and simple remedy for a complex difficulty.

In addition to its simplicity, rejection of social promotion has two other appealing aspects. First, passing children along without sufficient knowledge is obviously unfair to the children. Therefore, eliminating these phony promotions ought to be an improvement. Secondly, for anyone who is convinced that punishment is a solution to evils, this answer is ideal. Punish the child by making him or her repeat and the child will apply himself more intently, will learn the material, and will proceed onward. Unfortunately, as research shows, punishment is extremely difficult to harness. Often it has exactly the opposite effect from that intended.

On the negative side of eliminating social promotions, the considerable research on retention of students in the same grade usually indicates that this policy is harmful to children. This research combined with the absolute inanity of passing children along who cannot cope with the next grade, produces the logical conclusion that neither retaining the child in the same class nor social promotion is a satisfactory answer. If a child enters school behind most other children, or later falls behind, that pupil needs special attention to make up for what is missing. In most instances, that cannot happen merely by requiring the student to sit in the same classroom for a second (or third) year. The teacher in this second year has the same difficulties as that of the instructor in the previous year except that one or more additional ill prepared students are also in attendance. The difficulty increases, if after two attempts, the child is still deficient but is physically much more mature than the other members of the class.

Schools that try to eliminate social promotions often include extra schooling in summer school and this addition is certainly valuable. These children undoubtedly need the additional aid. In reality, they usually need more than is available. They require individual attention and may have needed it since the first day they came into the schoolroom. Only individualized instruction can have any hope of effectively bringing most of these children into the mainstream. The enormity of the problem in today's schools eliminates the possibility of giving all these students individualized instruction by a human teacher.

That discipline problems are rampant and cause disorder in schools should surprise no one. Everybody tries to protect his or her own self-worth. When protection is impossible in the usual ways, other means are used. Expressing utter contempt for education is a form of ego preservation. If education is valueless, failing the educational system cannot impinge on self-esteem. Unfortunately, the students who use this disruptive strategy need jobs when they leave school. The technological revolution in the workplace continues with accelerating speed, and education becomes ever more important. These pupils stumble from classrooms without skills and with few prospects except for menial jobs. These are the students who are potentially future welfare recipients as many of them are being supported by welfare payments to their parents today. In time, children of these frustrated pupils will be confronted with similar dilemmas. Without a fundamental revamping of education, the results will be the same.

Reformers outside education talk about needed social changes today. They often suggest replacing welfare with "workfare." Under "workfare" everybody on welfare would be forced to take a job after an initial period. Regrettably, it will be impossible to carry out these changes on a wide scale unless students are educated enough to hold jobs. Today's quandary is often not that people want to avoid work but that they cannot find a job.

Reformers within education tout a solution: "excellence." *A Nation At Risk* supported the need for excellence in education. This has been a constant rallying point among reform-minded educators in recent years. They maintain that all students must participate in improved schooling, and that standards for everybody must be raised, including those of slower pupils. Unfortunately that ideal isn't being met. Bottom-track students are being included in name only. School authorities have changed the types of courses making it appear that the poorer students are gaining. In their zeal to have students progress through the system and then to graduate, schools play semantic games with class names instead of making beneficial changes. The result is a mishmash of virtually worthless courses, all sufficiently anemic that even students who cannot read can pass them. For these courses, schools spew out credits with as much value toward graduation as those given for advanced mathematics or science. By this subterfuge of authorities, students accumulate enough credits to graduate. That "accomplishment" delights administrators.

Consequently, slow students stumble along and continue to take poor courses. Many drop out, sometimes because of their own discouragement at being a "dumb" kid. Even when they do manage to finish school they are woefully undereducated. Consequently, though they receive a high school diploma, they have learned little. This ridiculous practice allows American schools to graduate a higher percentage of students from high schools than any other country including Germany and Japan. When these "graduates" enter the job market, however, industry finds them hopelessly unprepared. Companies must then provide remedial education for employees who have been in a system supposedly dedicated completely to their education for twelve years. Need for these remedial courses is a condemnation of schools. The worst part is that present remedial education programs can't possibly educate the illiterate youths and adults that schools are producing: the numbers are too massive.

Computerized Education

Computerized education will bring an improvement of gargantuan value for the nation and for millions of individuals: better education for slower students who suffer the worst deprivations under the present system.

Supporting the theoretical conclusion that computerized education can alleviate the monstrous problems of tracking are the results of the programs for at-risk students in Florida schools cited in Chapter 5. Although no one has analyzed the tracks of these students, many were probably in the bottom tracks, at least toward the end of their regular school careers. Students can't enter these programs unless they are behind appreciably in academic achievement.

An overriding difficulty in schools today is that millions of students are unable to read at a seventh grade level. Even in the dropout programs in Florida, many potential candidates fail to qualify because of an inability to read well enough.

Another smaller but graphic tragedy, the sinking of the Titanic, provides an analogy. The school system has rammed an iceberg, and authorities struggle to keep the music playing while the ship sinks deeper into the unforgiving depths of illiteracy. Obviously, schools today are unable to teach all students to read at a suitable level since millions of present and former students remain illiterate. Students fall behind in the first or second grade because they don't learn to read. Catching up is hopeless. Somehow the schools must stop the gaping leak by improving reading skills. With today's system, however, they have about as much chance of success as did the captain of the first Titanic.

Computers can teach almost all children to read, even those who are severely handicapped. When every student in every classroom can read, American education will have undergone a monumental metamorphosis.

Computers are being used in some places, especially in English as a Second Language programs, to teach reading to children. The software allows the child to repeat the words and phrases and to have the pronunciation corrected by the machine. Adult programs also teach reading with excellent results. Annabell Thomas provides an example. She was unable to read despite her years in the New York City school system. In its issue of November 16, 1992, *The Wall Street Journal* carried her story. After leaving school, she had been taught by tutors and had enrolled in library literacy programs and adult education classes trying to overcome her handicap. Nonetheless, she never learned to read. Finally, Ms. Thomas, now 56, enrolled in a computer program and was taught to read and write by a computer.[6]

Computers are notably effective with slower students because the machines have the vital characteristic of unlimited patience. This trait is necessary in someone teaching a subject demanding frequent repetition and painstaking attention to details that are unnoticed by readers but frustrate non-readers. Computers can teach reading using either phonics or whole language learning or both, if one doesn't work well.

An unbiased onlooker, uninvolved in education, has to wonder, "What is going on? Why are millions of students like Jimmy Wedmore, the General Motors employee mentioned in Chapter 1, and Annabell Thomas unable to master basic skills when subsequent results prove they can learn? Why aren't schools using tested and effective methods of instruction? Why are only a handful of at-risk students profiting from what computers can accomplish while countless others remain uneducated? Why are our schools ignoring computers and trashing the lives of millions by allowing them to remain illiterate?"

Since computers can teach reading and language to students at every level and with any background, they can go far toward overcoming the years that intellectually deprived students have spent in school with no results. Computers could do what is now unthinkable, and could do it rapidly. They could effectively wipe out illiteracy in the nation. When this happens, poor students will have made a beginning. The school Titanic will have its gaping hole of poor reading skills plugged. Then the rest of the boat can be repaired. All children can become educated.

When computers are finally allowed to teach, "dumb" kids will begin to understand that they can learn and can become "smart" kids. After that, schools will be totally unlike present institutions with their large numbers of unlearned and unresponsive youth. Present students will profit, but their children will be the foremost beneficiaries. That next generation will grow up in a totally different home environment. They won't begin school burdened by a belief that education is only for others. Children from these homes will know that their parents received an education and they can do the same. Their educated parents will insist on it.

Chapter 11

Educating Brighter Students

*T*homas Edison had an unusual academic career. He started school when he was seven years old. Three months later the schoolmaster expelled him. "Retarded" was the master's chilling diagnosis. Fortunately for that school dropout, a private tutor was available: his mother. She took on the task of trying to impart knowledge to this apparent failure. For three years she was his teacher. Edison in later years said of his mother, "She instilled in me the love and purpose of learning." When he was ten, this tutor gave him an elementary physical science book. Young Edison read it avidly, and the world was forever changed.

Edison's experience in education was extreme. He was, however, neither the first nor the last talented youth to appear out of step with ordinary procedures and to cause consternation among teachers.

Since bright students can master lessons easily, they should have little difficulty. Learning should be enjoyable for everyone but should be particularly pleasurable for those who are unusually intelligent. Buoyed by their strong curiosity, they should pass through their schooling with few snags. This doesn't always happen. Many students with a high I.Q. fail to achieve their academic potential. A surprising number of those who drop out of school are above average in intelligence and are capable of doing the work necessary to graduate. At times, up to 40 percent of dropouts are enrolled in college-preparation courses. Their elders find it easy to issue platitudes and to say they should remain in school, but tens of thousands of brighter students aren't listening. They leave school before graduating.

Talented students may face a variety of obstacles. As happened to Edison, sometimes their good qualities are unappreciated. They can be difficult to teach, and at times instructors find it easier to avoid stimulating their intellectual powers. Moreover, teachers often lack sufficient time to fathom the real strengths and weaknesses and needs of their pupils.

Many smarter students have a characteristic that is negative but can be a positive if cultivated properly. They are easily bored. They find that learning is an intriguing challenge, and they work diligently to succeed. When they reach one goal, they need another or tedium will follow. Often subsequent challenges are delayed because other students in the class need more time to learn. The interest of those who have immediately understood wanes rapidly. This ability of bright pupils to grasp new material quickly can be used positively if sufficient challenges can be provided. Boredom is distasteful, and bright students will avoid it by taking up new undertakings. Keeping these pupils gainfully occupied is difficult, however, when twenty or thirty other students in the same class also need the attention of the teacher.

This propensity to become bored can be a decided negative. Sometimes their failure to progress rapidly hinders only themselves. At times, however, they turn their talents to disruption, and others also suffer. These bright youths find an antidote for their boredom by baiting and upsetting their teachers.

Slower students use disruptions to defend their self-worth when they fall behind. They act out to cover their frustration. Bright students use disruptions to dispel their boredom when they can't go ahead. Just as schools must often bear responsibility for episodes of acting out by slower students, schools must take some blame for bright students who act out.

Unfortunately for schools, the native ability of bright students often helps them devise ingenious ways to disrupt classes and upset teachers. Authorities, faced with unacceptable behavior, tend to blame the pupil. Edison's schoolmaster felt completely justified in his appraisal of this baffling student.

Not every child with higher intelligence, of course, is a problem for teachers. Nonetheless, many bright students who conform to the system do not meet their potential because they are seldom challenged in ordinary courses. Schools must establish curriculum requirements at a level that most students can reach, but below the capabilities of truly bright students. Their talents lie unused. They suffer, but the nation also suffers.

"Honors" programs are often set up for these pupils. Nonetheless, American schools lag behind schools in other nations as shown in Chapter 1. Therefore, many Honors programs fail to carry all bright students to their full potential. Honors courses have additional problems. Acceptance into them is often based on success with an I.Q. test, or some similar accomplishment. Intelligence is not, however, a unitary trait that is easily quantified despite the ease of scoring standard I.Q. tests.

Even after being accepted into Honors courses, students may fail to reach their full potential. Certain students with extraordinary talents in one area may be held back in that subject by other bright students with different talents or interests. Also, teachers may be ill equipped to help those with superior qualities. One education official told me that the major problem in her highly respected Honors Program was the school's inability to give more training to instructors.

Even with exceptionally fine Honors programs, other difficulties can still thwart very talented students. They may be overlooked when their outstanding qualities are specific. A unique brilliance in one area may receive less attention than a series of high grades. Sometimes real genius can be well hidden and require unbiased judgment and patience to bring it out. When hidden, it is easily overlooked and could be lost. Perhaps Thomas Edison might still have achieved success if his mother had allowed the opinion of the schoolmaster to go uncontested, perhaps not. Probably his self-esteem, at least, would have been injured.

Computers can be programmed to spot exceptional talent in one subject or in many. They can compare age and subject matter finished at the conclusion of every section, and they can note when a student goes through a subject faster than expected. This could represent outstanding talent, which is easily quantified and recorded by computers. At least, it would show that additional investigation was warranted. High ability students need to be located, encouraged, and given the chance to proceed as far as their talents can take them.

Even a recognized "slow" student may also be a brighter student whose intelligence is misunderstood by instructors. Being bright doesn't eliminate psychological scars that may have been inflicted in home situations or elsewhere. Students with those scars may have difficulty showing their talents.

Teachers in computer schools will have more time to get to know students well and to assess them more accurately as I will show in Chapters 18 to 20. In the at-risk programs in Florida, an invaluable part of the programs is the personal attention that teachers can give students.

Bright students may encounter another hindrance. Sometimes topics intrigue them before they reach the classes in school. At times they will delve into these subjects but without a coordinated plan for learning. They stumble around and fail to become truly knowledgeable in the subject. Being bright, however, they absorb enough to be totally bored when they encounter the course in school. With computers, students who finish one area can go on to another immediately. This opportunity to advance rapidly will allow them to enter many studies at a much earlier age. As challenges continue in their ongoing courses, they will be less likely to go off into other subjects by themselves. Even if they do, they can pass rapidly through the basic material when they finally meet the course in school. Computers will be unconcerned by numbers of days spent in classes. They can present new challenges and advanced material whenever it is helpful.

That powerful innate desire to learn that is obvious in bright children will trigger vast gains through full use of computers. Later, as adults, these bright students may increase the total knowledge in the world. These are pupils that society needs to encourage and to bring along at a fast pace. Despite their advanced learning, maturation of their social skills will continue in the usual way. These children will remain with others in their age group.

With computer instruction, learning possibilities for students can be expanded beyond what is conceivable in present courses. Since classes can be individualized for each student according to interest and ability, limits will vanish. Students will have the prodigious resources of constantly developing computer programs. Moreover, as software is being developed, scholars in various fields can join programmers to provide avenues for exceptional learning for the brightest pupils.

Many other learning opportunities will also flourish. An example is study of foreign languages. One prominent shortcoming of American education has always been the weakness in teaching a second or third language when students are very young and adept at acquiring linguistic skills. Not only are languages usually available only in later years, they are often taught by Americans who have an accented pronunciation and less than complete ease with a language they learned primarily in school. With computers teaching foreign languages, instruction can begin at an early age, perhaps in kindergarten. The pronunciation that the child hears will be that of speakers for whom it is the first language, and who know and speak it exactly.

For highly intelligent students, computers will provide ideal conditions. These pupils will be able to advance at their individual pace starting when they study basic subjects. This capability alone will mean incredible advances over present time schedules. At-risk students in Florida's dropout prevention programs sometimes finish two or three years of work in one year. Imagine what highly intelligent students could accomplish in one year or five years with complete computerized education! Without the constraints found in present classrooms, many bright students could finish their basic class materials in fewer than the twelve years they squander in schools today. They would then spend the remaining years in other studies. If schools today, advanced their better students more rapidly, they would face a jarring dilemma: nothing would remain for the pupils after completing the requirements of even an upgraded curriculum. In computerized education, advanced lessons will always be available. When they are ready, students will have almost unlimited access to additional learning. Few boundaries will hinder their curiosity and intellectual prowess. Brighter students are those who will take fullest advantage of the capacity of computers to foster self-directed learning. Consequently, many will find an area that corresponds to their talents as Edison found his book on physical sciences.

Brighter students will also benefit because teachers will have more time in computer schools. Instructors enjoy interacting with intelligent pupils. In computer schools, teachers will not only be able to interact but will also be able to generate new learning experiences for top students. Enthusiasm of teachers about their subjects will continue to rub off on pupils, and especially on the smarter ones. With their additional time, mentors will be better able to emulate Edison's mother and instill more powerfully "the love and purpose of learning."

I will show in Chapters 19 that a vital and enormously productive part of computerized education will be seminars and workshops that teachers will conduct. These learning activities will be further enhanced because regular classes will not require uninterrupted attendance. Groups of students from different schools will be able to attend workshops or seminars for a week or longer. The whole emphasis could be centered on a specific area intriguing to participants. New methods that creative teachers will devise to aid bright children can't even be imagined now.

Since computers will have modems, students will further their education by interacting with their peers throughout the nation and world. They will have telephonic access to the Internet and to vast stores of information in today's databases. Teachers in their seminars and workshops will encourage this use of the learning opportunities on the World Wide Web, or its later adaptations.

When pupils have reached a defined level in their own schools, they will be able to enter regional, national, or international groups through the phone lines. These opportunities will provide them with additional stimuli to advance, and ideas on which to build. All students will find new and enhancing enticements for continued learning from these exchanges, but the brightest will profit most.

Even games can be used by brighter students to sharpen skills. New games requiring intellectual acumen will be developed for computers. Students will participate but only if they keep up with their other scholastic activities. Inter-scholastic competitions based on intellectual endeavors might someday take place and excite other pupils to watch play action through their computers. The interest that was generated by the chess match between Bobby Fischer and Boris Spassky in 1992 may have presaged that possibility. Thousands of subscribers to *Prodigy*, a national computer network, followed a move-by-move account accompanied by a commentary by chess experts. In 1996 and 1997, the chess matches between Gary Kasparov and Deep Blue, an IBM computer, were again carried to thousands of fans, this time through the Internet.

Chess is viewed by critics as a tediously slow game that could never develop a major following in America. In Russia, however, where a widespread knowledge of the game exists, public matches fascinate intellectuals. Perhaps new computer games might be developed that could rival the excitement of watching a football game for at least some students.

Certain students will find exciting challenges in writing computer programs. Competition will add a further stimulus. Students will be presented with a problem, perhaps unsolved until then, and asked to find a programming solution. At other times, they will be presented with software in existence and asked to find an improvement. Criteria for success might be speed or reduced numbers of instructions. Students will submit their solutions, which will be judged by computers. These competitions could be national or international and will present additional learning opportunities because all solutions will be available to participants. Students will be able, at their leisure, to ponder how others attacked and unraveled the problem.

In computerized education, few limits will impede advanced students. Vast reservoirs of knowledge will be readily available. Computers will not only provide access to those storehouses of learning but will also guide and prepare students to use them well.

Although all students will benefit from computerized education, bright students will probably reap the most impressive gains.

Chapter 12

Fulfilling the Need to Succeed

*A*ctors and actresses obviously need success. When they don't achieve it, the outcome is predictable. Visualize an actor giving a one-person performance before a live audience. Imagine that at the conclusion the spectators fail to applaud and parade out of the theater unconcerned with what they had seen. The actor would be devastated. If a smaller and smaller audience showed up on the following nights and the reaction was always the same—dead silence—only an unusual performer would dare to continue. Incidentally, it would be useless for the authorities of the theater to exhort him to try harder.

Making a protracted effort without success or prospect of achievement is guaranteed to bring discouragement and frustration. This principle is apparent with actors and actresses but applies to everyone, everywhere, at every age level. Definitions of success and acceptable time frames may differ. Nonetheless, the basic need to succeed is present in everyone. If it is never fulfilled in a specific endeavor, further attempts in that area will eventually cease.

Students who had learned in school but then suffered an injury that lessened their intellectual powers can remember that they once learned. Despite difficult odds, they may continue to make efforts to learn again because they have experienced earlier successes. Adults can sometimes strive for long range goals without immediate gratification. They have reached earlier objectives. Consequently, they believe they can again succeed even if the reward is delayed. If, however, they lose that hope or belief, they will find it impossible to continue striving.

Millions of students have never succeeded. They are and have always been behind. If they ever thought they could learn, they lost that idea quickly. Teachers are faced with the impossible problem of getting them to work at their studies, but the pupils can't do this until they know they can succeed. An unending cycle cripples their schooling. They don't succeed; this failure destroys their will to keep trying; they can't succeed if they don't try.

No exit from this cycle is possible for most of these failing students today. It is useless for authorities to exhort them to try harder. The result is frustration for teachers, students, and officials.

Instructors know the value of success and want to find ways to make slow students succeed. They can't be faulted if they don't achieve their goal. Their time is limited, and they must attempt to help all students at the same time. Sometimes they have students who are unable to read and thus have no hope at all. It is counter productive for a teacher to try to encourage poor students by telling them that they have done well but then give them a D or F at the end of the semester. Students realize they are deficient when they see their grade and may consider their instructor untruthful.

Authorities at times hope that the objective of being educated will stimulate hard work by students. The status or high value of the goal is unable to induce efforts. Many of us might find the prospect of being a high paid major league ball player an inspiring goal. If, however, the local Little League ball club had only used us as a third string replacement and the high school team had spurned our ardent advances, our enthusiasm would dissipate. Long range goals need intermediate success to endure.

When students are unable to get passing grades, they are understandably unmoved by the contention that good grades will mean more pay later. As I noted above, in the Florida at-risk programs, students were indifferent about graduation before using computers. The potential benefits were meaningless. Even if they wanted to qualify, they couldn't. When they began to learn in the computer classes and felt they might be able to graduate, their outlook changed dramatically. They began to work zealously toward that goal. Future potential gain from a diploma became a driving motivation because it was coupled with present achievements.

This inability of schools to enable poor students to succeed is another crucial reason educational reforms have had only minimal effect despite monumental efforts in the past fifteen years.

Role of Computers

Computers can break this impasse. They will enable every student, without exception, to attain success in school. They can provide this universal success by dividing lessons into segments—as small as needed to guarantee that every student can always accomplish something. The result will be one small achievement followed by another and another. Each accomplishment, no matter how insignificant it may seem to onlookers, is vital to that one individual and encourages him or her to continue.

Pupils who are unfamiliar with success in academic activities tend to disbelieve even the possibility that they can do well. They need to be told immediately when they have succeeded, and computers can do this easily.

Knowledge of personal success is rewarding to the student, and a well-documented psychological principle says, "Whatever is rewarded tends to be repeated." Each activity that is rewarded will lead to another effort, and the computer can ensure that this additional effort will again result in success.

Although segments can be as small as necessary, they will differ according to student needs. Software can adjust lessons according to many variables including the rate of progression of the pupil. Bright students will remain stimulated though they can speed through sections that might be difficult for slower students. They will quickly reach challenges appropriate for their abilities and will be encouraged to go on. Success energizes everyone.

Computers can be programmed to enhance rewards by adding a bit of pizzazz when appropriate. Rewards are part of the success of video and computer games. When a player makes a spectacular laser shot and destroys the dastardly incoming alien spaceship, the machine may acknowledge the feat in many ways. These rewards may seem unsophisticated, but properly used, they are important elements in the fascination that video games have exerted on everybody who has enjoyed them. I remember waiting in an out-of-the-way airport many years ago in the early days of video games before they had become commonplace. Flight delays were extended, and ways to kill time were scarce in that airport on that day. As a result, businessmen began to try to help Mario rescue a princess. They quickly became entranced by the game, and a line formed. Delivering an imaginary princess from an equally unreal adversary was insignificant in the lives of the players. Nonetheless, these supposedly unsophisticated rewards were enough to keep the businessmen pumping quarters into a hunk of inanimate machinery. They seemed chagrined when they ran out of quarters and had to hand the machine on to the next one in line. I know I was, when my horde of coins was exhausted. Many school programs would delight if they could develop a similar intensity by students to master academic subjects even for brief periods of time.

One element of rewards can multiply or diminish their value: the speed with which they are delivered. The closer the connection between the action and the reward, the more valuable and more effective is the reward. Conversely, the value is diminished as the time between the action and its outcome is extended.

In today's schools, immediate rewards are infrequent. Whenever teachers give a written test, it must be collected and corrected before the student knows the result. Prolonged delay of rewards is evident in grades given at the end of a semester. Students must work toward their grades for weeks before they learn the results.

In class recitations an immediate acknowledgement of a correct answer meets the criterion for speed. Ordinarily, however, only a few students can seize the available opportunities on any single occasion. Except for these public sessions, an interval always interrupts the action and its effect.

Just as in video games, the reward for succeeding in a segment in computerized education is rapid. A computer can test frequently with no difficulty. The machine can evaluate answers instantaneously and immediately notify the student. Delays are virtually nonexistent. If the results are unfavorable, the computer might even legitimately accept blame for failing to explain the material well. It can also emphasize any small accomplishments. Then it will begin to teach again what the pupil missed. As the student progresses, praise will always follow quickly.

Accolades bestowed by the machine can be augmented by another important reward: the approval of a human teacher. Although not as prompt as that of the machine, it will add a valuable human element. This will be discussed below when speaking of teachers in Chapter 19.

Rewards and Goals

Teachers have always understood the importance of rewards in classrooms. They hang good papers on the wall for everyone to see; they add well deserved complimentary comments on a composition before they return it; they are delighted when they can give a high grade. Computers will add nothing new since rewards have always been an integral part of education. Computers, however, will make them more closely connected with their cause. They will allow them to be universal and available to everyone. Rewards will have different degrees of subtlety, but they will be frequent, legitimate, and rapid. That combination will always generate results.

Continual lack of classroom accomplishment weighs heavily on youngsters, and they revolt against the school system. Success has different forms. To a school authority, academic accomplishments are the hallmarks of achievement. Some students find success through their athletic abilities. Those who have neither athletic nor academic achievements still crave success. They must seek it elsewhere. Their inclinations can run counter to what authorities believe is ideal. Graffiti sprayed on a clean wall may appear ugly to a neat and prim authority figure. It might be beautiful to a youth who is rewarded when he sees an immediate and dramatic change caused by his efforts. Watching a disliked teacher become irritated and exasperated can be a form of reward. The upset teacher might reject it as an admirable accomplishment, but the reactions of the teacher and fellow students could be highly stimulating for the perpetrator. The immediacy of that reward makes it a more effective prod for future actions aimed at a similar result. Society, schools, and teachers will benefit when students achieve success by schoolwork rather than by creating disturbances.

In the Florida at-risk programs, teachers are unanimous in their appreciation of the value of success to students. Accomplishment of a task is vital in changing bored, disruptive, and seemingly unconcerned classroom occupants into determined learners. Once students find they can achieve success, they seek and find other avenues of academic attainment. The at-risk students keep close track of how many segments they have finished each day. Teachers can even encourage a bit of bragging and listen attentively. They can honestly add their own praise for these accomplishments, and these compliments delight and further stimulate the students.

While computerized education can assure that every student without exception can succeed, our present system can never achieve that ideal. Until pupils can enjoy accomplishments in their studies, Herculean efforts by millions of dedicated teachers and school officials to make them appreciate education must remain futile.

Chapter 13

Using Educational Research

*T*hose who are attempting to improve education face a difficulty that has afflicted schools since long before the current crisis: successful research has generated only tepid follow-through. Scientists have carried out many studies to unearth more effective ways of teaching. Better methodologies have been uncovered, but they have resulted in little change in instruction by teachers and thus few improvements in education.

Classic examples illustrate this phenomenon. As far back as 1924, researchers discovered that testing could have a more important duty than merely ascertaining the amount of lesson material that a student has retained. Effectively used, it can also serve as a valuable teaching aid. Despite a lapse of over seventy years since the first study, and succeeding reports that indicated the same outcome, many teachers think of testing only in a traditional way. Instructors have good reasons why they hesitate to make broader use of tests. It places an additional burden on them because they must not only devise the tests but must also spend precious hours of their limited time correcting them. This time expenditure obviously becomes more burdensome than can be justified at some point, whatever the intrinsic benefit from testing.

Evidence for the value of another methodology can be traced back even further than that on testing. This finding has been known for over a century and has been used in Russia, but it has never generated much enthusiasm in American schools. This technique is the so-called "Spacing Effect." Studies have shown that presentations of material for learning are more beneficial if the material is spaced rather than massed. For an equal amount of study time, a lesson taught in small sections instead of in massed amounts is more effective. Many teachers are unaware of the phenomenon and its corroborating research.[1]

These two examples illustrate a fundamental difficulty for education: research findings are unused in classrooms. This lack of follow-up is easily understandable. If classroom instruction is to incorporate research, each teacher must carry out the new method. Here, again, the unique characteristics and teaching agendas found in millions of instructors create insurmountable roadblocks. This problem has been pointed out in the difficulties of creating software. It will arise again with the difficulties of replication in Chapter 25. Teachers have their own way of teaching and they must evaluate new methods in the context of their instruction.

In addition, other obstacles also impede the successful use of research. Obviously, before any teacher can use a finding, he or she must know of its existence and must be convinced of its efficacy. Neither is automatic. Many teachers don't become aware of specific educational research. Even when they do know of a study, a conviction that it is suitable may be elusive since research often brings results that can be interpreted differently when used by different teachers with varied skills.

Even if teachers think new ideas will help, they also must know how to apply the findings in the classroom and must remember the research when the proper circumstances are present. Overlaying these difficulties is another that accompanies human nature in every activity: inertia. It is easier to do something as it has been done before instead of undertaking a new procedure.

Research results will be easily brought into classrooms with computerized education. The two examples of frequent testing and spacing will pose no problems for software developers. They will build a series of tests into their programs to make sure that the student understands the material, but also to enhance learning. Neither testing nor correction of the exercises will be difficult for the machines. Spacing, also, can be easily put in place through software.

Computer programmers can use past and future research. Millions of teachers will not be required to learn about it nor to try to put it into practice in their unique situations with their special talents. Only scholars and other experts employed by software companies will need to be aware of it. These authorities can study research to decide how it will be used effectively. They can then pass their conclusions with suggestions for implementation to programmers, who will incorporate the ideas in software and present the results for further comments and evaluation.

When this analysis is completed, the new advancements will be made available immediately through modems to software throughout the country. Upon receipt in schools, the new research will become part of programs then in use. It will immediately enhance the software of every student studying the course. As pupils use the new programs, the familiar computer feedback will again provide benefits. Learning results will be returned via the modems to the programmers and educational experts. After sufficient data have been received, those who are assisting the programmers will be able to decide if the new methods are effective.

Where results are less than absolutely positive, changes can be made easily and quickly. Under present conditions, when a new method is devised, a researcher will try it out in a limited area. After the necessary trials, results can be published in a journal. This procedure may have consumed years from the first idea to its publication when other researchers receive the information. If the results seem promising, others may embark on their own studies of the new method. They will often try variations. Their results may corroborate the first studies or may add other questions. More time has passed. A slow process then becomes even less productive because results have little impact in classrooms.

In computerized education, when programmers have different possible approaches, they will be able to try one method in some schools, and simultaneously, another in equivalent locations. Results can be compared to find the better teaching method. Companies producing software can continually upgrade their programming.

Computers will be the source of new investigations. Researchers will accumulate vast quantities of valuable data with little additional expenditure of machine time. They will pass their conclusions to programmers who will be able to upgrade and improve their software.

Since computers, under the direction of companies developing software, will be responsible for research, the numbers of individuals working in separate schools and developing projects will be lessened. That may be thought of by some as a regrettable result but is no different from what happens frequently in scientific fields today.

In other industries, technical research is carried out in large companies with ample staffs. Sometimes, more people create additional chances that a detrimental bureaucracy will arise and hinder research. Nonetheless, well-trained staffs working on a coordinated project can hasten scientific advances. Benefits are apparent from the technological advances that are made continually in companies throughout the world. Relatively few solitary workers make major scientific breakthroughs today. Research can be done more efficiently and can be carried out more readily as a group undertaking. Ideas of individuals will always be essential, but larger staffs with greater resources will carry them forward. Software companies will use educational researchers exactly as other technological companies employ experts in their fields.

As a result of improved research, teaching will become more of a science than an art. Education will assume its rightful position among the sciences.

Computers can add another element that is connected with research. The machines can use varying methods with different students. Teaching styles can change according to the needs of pupils. The speed of computers will enable analysis to be made not only of patterns of learning throughout school systems but also of separate students. The machines can keep track of what type of teaching is effective in a specific environment and watch for similar circumstances. When these conditions appear, the method that is probably the best can be used. If it is unsuccessful with a student, other varieties of computer teaching can be tried until an effective one is found. The students will always be treated as unique persons, but their similarities are also important.

The speed and analytical capability of computers can be used to discover and address basic shortcomings in any lesson. Computers can be programmed to detect problems and to allow students to make their difficulties known to research staff who can carry out further study. Improvements in software will again result.

Computerized education will mark the beginning of massive new studies of teaching methods that are impossible today. The final outcome will be that improved and expanded research in education will not lie fallow in technical journals. Rather, it will make the jump from pure theory to classrooms where it can affect learning. In the future, research results will bring better teaching, and students and schools will benefit.

Chapter 14

Directing Multimedia

Some teachers make lessons interesting; some don't. Those who are skilled in theatrics have an advantage. They can conduct classes that grab and hold the attention of their students. Since no one can require teachers to add this talent to their teaching repertoire, schools have to adopt the attitude that children must accept teaching as it is, even if it is sometimes uninteresting. After all, students are the ones benefiting from education. They ought to be willing to put up with a little discomfort in return for what they are receiving.

This idealistic but naive attitude means little in a classroom. Whenever students are bored, learning is lessened appreciably. In the mass media world of today, instructors face an additional obstacle when they try to keep the attention of students: they must indirectly compete with highly talented actors and writers who bombard pupils with entertaining films and TV programs outside school hours. These shows keep the attention of pupils with material that is cleverly written and superbly delivered. The contrast between these professional media presentations and normal classes increases the apathy that students suffer. Children have grown accustomed to being entertained. They are not at fault because they are presented with a constant outpouring of technically magnificent programs outside school.

Nor is it the fault of teachers when their attempts to compete fall short. They chose to be teachers, not actors or actresses. They can't be criticized for failing to excel in knowledge and in delivery skills at the same time. Even writers and actors aren't skilled in both. Nonetheless, teaching must contend against these clever shows that students see daily on television and in movies.

Use of Audiovisual Programs

Teachers sometimes improve their classes by incorporating audiovisual, or A-V, materials into their lessons. These programs make use of films, recordings and video productions to instruct, and many of these displays can compete technically with the media fare that students see outside the classroom. A-V lessons can enhance education, but this technology furnishes the same difficult challenges to teachers that confront them when they use computers:

- They must schedule times to show films or videos.
- They must ensure that the necessary teaching materials and equipment will be available.
- They must at times contend with mechanical problems in projectors or video machines.
- They must harmonize the audiovisual lesson with their teaching skills and integrate it with requirements of the curriculum.
- They must provide the audiovisual display simultaneously to all their students, although the pupils are not equally prepared to learn.
- They can't identify the individual needs of all their pupils, and some of their students might learn more if certain parts were repeated.
- Usually, they can't repeat the showing for part of the class while the rest moves on to other lessons, and they can't provide the same show again for all pupils without boring many of them.
- Another difficulty that is absolutely insurmountable often occurs: on the day that the presentation is made, some students may be ill and absent and miss the film or video.

Teachers who have difficulties are not alone. Companies that produce audiovisual materials for schools labor under the same handicaps that confront firms developing computer programs for schools today. Their products must be filtered through the instructional agendas of individual teachers and must fit these unique teaching styles. Purchase of audiovisual programs is dependent upon the desires and requirements of teachers, not on the inherent worth of the program. It is of little value to producers to design superb A-V teaching tools if teachers don't buy them.

The consequence of these difficulties for teachers and manufacturers of audiovisual materials is inevitable. Despite their many valuable features, A-V presentations have been unable to make significant improvements in education after many years of use.

Multimedia—The New Audiovisual Experience

When personal computers first appeared, writing and figures on the screen could only be in one color. Users chose among white, green or amber when they selected their monitor. Forever afterward, the color of their characters on the eternal black background of that screen was unchanged.

The history of computers is replete with rapid improvements. Those original restrictions lasted only briefly. Manufacturers quickly introduced full color monitors, and viewing became more pleasant and less tiring to eyes. Movement was always possible on computer screens, but originally it was restricted to simple creations of programmers like stick figures or bouncing balls. As computer memories grew more massive, color pictures of photographic quality were practical, and movement of images improved significantly. The addition of sound provided a further enhancement. Today computers can reproduce films with precision.

Color, sound, and movement—under the total direction of a computer—are the components of multimedia. As an educational tool, it can make learning more appealing and more effective than ever previously imagined. It will enable education to compete with the outstanding shows that are produced on TV and in theaters. Computers can control multimedia for each student on his or her own screen and can integrate the technology into lessons. Multimedia has all the valuable features of audiovisuals, but it adds at least three additional benefits for education:

1. Individualized Instruction

Many difficulties that teachers now confront when they use A-V shows will disappear because of a computer's ability to provide lessons geared to the precise needs of each student. This individualizing will begin before the presentation is made. Computers will often be able to determine what type of multimedia presentation is appropriate for a particular pupil. The material will be delivered when the child is prepared to receive it. Either during or immediately after a presentation, the machine will test the student and evaluate results. If something important was missed, all or part of the presentation can be repeated. Sometimes computers will be able to provide a different exhibit to overcome the deficiency.

2. Use of Presentations of Varying Lengths

Another major advantage of multimedia over today's audiovisual format is the ease with which it can be employed in lessons. Teachers today are unable to interject short film clips to accentuate a point. Scheduling and setting up the equipment waste valuable teaching time. With multimedia, however, it will be equally possible for the computer to provide one minute or one hour of instruction using films or clips and to use them as frequently as will be helpful. No tedious delays will bore students while separate equipment is set up, and no distracting transitions from one medium to another will hinder learning.

3. Interaction Between Student and Computer

Despite the use of moving pictures, audiovisual materials have a static feature. The content of a movie or a video is unchangeable in the classroom and students cannot interact with it except in a passive role. Computers eliminate these constraints. The sequence of multimedia displays can easily be altered. Computers are able to adjust programs according to the reactions of pupils. Students and machines will respond to each other, and each response will stimulate further interaction.

Presentations will never be fixed and unchanging. A student will be able to ask questions pertinent to the material being taught. The machine will answer, and perhaps use the question and its response to make or enhance a point with a different display or film clip or demonstration. The machine may propose questions of its own to involve the student more fully during the show. The reactions of the pupil will determine the direction the computer will take to reach the goal of teaching the essential material while the graphics entice and involve the student. Interchange between child and computer will allow pupils to participate intensely while they learn. This capability, of course, differs from today's audiovisual presentations where interaction between students and the teacher must occur before or after the show. At either time, the teacher is forced to confront the always-present difficulty of interacting with many different students simultaneously.

This interactive capability of multimedia will open many new avenues to learning. Lessons that incorporate the latest equipment can be provided, and students will feel as if they were operating the machines. They will receive responses from the computer simulation as they would from the actual gear.

A simple example is use of telescopes or microscopes, which will behave as if they were present on the student's desk. Pupils will be able to focus and zoom in on features that they are examining as if they were peering into an actual microscope or telescope before them. Concurrent with the displays will be explanations, both verbal and written.

Additional pertinent benefits will follow. Instruments will always be up-to-date, and every student will have a separate piece of equipment. Today, the expense precludes those possibilities. Even if schools were wealthy enough to afford hardware for each pupil, finding and retaining qualified teachers would be impossible. Moreover, computers will have their usual advantage of personal attention and instruction for each student.

The federal government has been able to make extensive use of the interactive features of computers in education. The conclusion of one review from the Department of Defense is worth noting. Researchers examined forty-seven studies. They summarized results saying:

> Interactive videodisc instruction was more effective the more the interactive features of the medium were used. It was equally effective for knowledge and performance outcomes. It was less costly than conventional instruction. Overall, interactive videodisc instruction demonstrated sufficient utility in terms of effectiveness, cost, and acceptance to recommend that it now be routinely considered and used in Defense training and education.[1]

Multimedia Today

Multimedia is in its infancy but is advancing rapidly. In January 1993, IBM emphasized the increasing importance of this new approach by forming a separate unit within the company to direct future developments. They named the new unit *Fireworks Partners*, an unusual name but appropriate as an indication of the possibilities in this field.

Multimedia programs available today give glimpses into the educational possibilities of the technology. Microsoft has brought out a program called Beethoven, an in-depth study of Beethoven's Ninth Symphony complete with laser duplication of the music, and accompanied by a measure-by-measure commentary from an expert on the composer. Explanations appear on the screen as the music is played. The disk includes an introduction to the musical structure of the piece and to the instruments that are used in the rendition, always with sound and video accompaniment. These features are enhanced with a history lesson on the social, cultural and political happenings that were taking place and influencing Beethoven as he composed this musical work. Viewers can move about in the program, unhampered by a predetermined arrangement. If a student is intrigued by one aspect, he or she could pursue that further. By adding appropriate testing, the program could allow great flexibility to the student's approach to learning but ensure that all important matter was covered. The interest generated when students follow their inclinations aids retention. Although this disk is intended for the general public it could easily fit into many school programs on music appreciation.

Although schools can adapt many programs for their use, most manufacturers direct their sales efforts at other markets, especially families. Companies thereby avoid the problems that software producers have encountered when they created software for classrooms. Nonetheless, these firms are aware of the educational possibilities of this technology. Microsoft, in the promotional piece advertising their multimedia encyclopedia maintains that, "It brings *learning* to life with words, images, animations, and sounds that work together to create a fascinating universe of knowledge. It sparks curiosity, opens the door to wonder, and starts a *learning* adventure that never ends." Later, the brochure adds, "It helps you find the joy of *learning*" (emphasis added).

Other Possible Uses of Multimedia

The full potential of interactive multimedia presentations is awesome. Even an old standby that has existed in various forms in education for centuries, lectures, can partake of its power. Although only a few people can speak with sufficient force, appeal, and wit to keep listeners spellbound, a few modern versions of that renowned orator of ancient times, Demosthenes, can be found among professional actors. They could be employed, and experts in the subject matter, aided by educators and others, could write their material.

Students will watch these presentations on their screens with the voice coming over their earphones. Frequency of talks will vary depending on subjects and pedagogical considerations, but when circumstances are opportune, an occasional professional lecture can be a valuable learning device. This technique is seldom used today in A-V displays. It would seem superfluous. Teachers also give oral presentations at times, and they might justifiably view use of professional speakers as unfair competition. These market limitations lessen the monetary incentives of companies to develop moving talks.

The listeners to the modern counterparts of the orators of old will enjoy added features undreamed of by the original speakers or their audiences. These modern lecturers will be integrated with the interactive capability of computers. A lecture will be carried for some minutes, and then pertinent film clips can be interjected to heighten interest. The computer will then return to the lecture. If the student doesn't understand something, he or she can interrupt the lecture or the film clip to ask a question or request more information. The machine will either provide information that was requested, or retain the question and return to it later. For a teacher to individualize a lecture in this way is impossible; for a computer it will be simple.

The powerful features of multimedia will be used in many subjects. A geography class can give pictures of the country and interviews with the people as ongoing parts of the presentation. These additions can be as frequent as helpful and will be integrated completely into the lesson.

History courses can provide accurate portrayals on film to accompany the bare facts of dates and events. Parts of historical movies could be culled, always under the direction of historians who could choose only the episodes that were accurate. Hollywood has magnificent technology but has a tendency to take liberties with historical facts. Multimedia presentations in schools will adopt only scenes that are accurate and helpful.

Science lessons will provide pictures to go with the scientific material that is taught. For example, on a lesson on electromagnetic forces, a film could reenact the original discovery of the phenomenon. Then additional clips could show actual uses of the principle as it evolved over many years. Finally, demonstration of present research will generate additional interest. Learning and retention will improve appreciably for all youngsters because the material will be presented in an engaging form.

Through these improvements, multimedia can eliminate the many shortcomings of A-V materials and present a new learning experience. Coming technical improvements in multimedia will dwarf even today's notable successes. The future will bring not only simple upgrades but also amazing new developments.

The Danger

The components that make up multimedia—sound, pictures, and animation—are the same elements that have always been present in audiovisual materials in classes. When A-V displays were first made available to schools, the potential value to learning seemed to be immense. The final result fell short of original hopes, and education improved only slightly. The same danger could sabotage multimedia. If schools try to use this new resource without complete computerized education, they will waste one more potent educational assistant. Without this computer direction, multimedia must remain in the same position as audiovisual materials today: a powerful tool with little effect in classrooms.

When, however, computers are allowed to direct multimedia, a new age in education will appear. This technology will make lessons come vibrantly alive. Future generations may look back on present teaching as we look back on the "little red schoolhouse." Since those impoverished one-room learning environments were the only possibilities in some areas, they were necessary, and they had to suffice at the time. Computers manipulating multimedia presentations were fantasies until recently. Before this, schools did well considering what they had. The old-fashioned one-room schoolhouse is now an anachronism. Schools without integrated computer and multimedia capabilities will arrive at the same status.

Since computerized education can captivate students, repeating a counsel of Plato many centuries ago is fitting:

> knowledge which is acquired under compulsion obtains no hold on the mind.... do not use compulsion, but let early education be a sort of amusement; you will then be better able to find out the natural bent.[2]

Plato would have been delighted by education capitalizing on the advantages of multimedia, which can amuse and fascinate students beyond anything he could have imagined.

Chapter 15

Eliminating Prejudice

*T*he differences between the memories in computers and those in humans are never more striking than when considering the genesis of prejudice or bigotry. Computers store only information. Human memories keep much more, including feelings. Software must tell computers what to retain. Any happening that occurs within the sensory range of humans may remain willy-nilly. Anything in a computer memory can be easily and completely erased. Information in minds can only be "forgotten." This forgetting may leave an influence on future actions, a hidden residual, which can be a cause of prejudice and a deterrent to its elimination.

Youths have memories that are especially receptive. Children absorb and retain learning, which remains immediately available to them throughout their lives. An adult requires no thought to answer "What is five times two?" No one has to think about how to ride a bicycle many years after first learning. Unfortunately, no conscious thought is needed to act on learned prejudices either.

During their early years, if persons or events suggest to children that people with other characteristics are inferior, they may carry that idea permanently because they cannot erase their memories. Years later their actions may be influenced by what they originally learned, or thought they learned, about different kinds of people.

Prejudiced adults may be unaware that anything is askew with their thinking. Almost everybody acknowledges that prejudice exists, but seldom does anyone admit that he or she is infected. Lewis Terman was cited previously with his comments about the genetic inferiority of immigrants. Terman would have denied that he was bigoted toward this class of people. He thought he was merely stating facts. Supposed "facts" form an almost impermeable shield that hides prejudice and enables bigots to deny personal culpability. Denial is intensified because of the origin of the prejudice: happenings long forgotten but not completely erased.

Fervent and sincere disavowal of prejudice by those who are tainted is neither uncommon nor surprising, but the denial changes neither the condition nor the consequences. Teachers resent accusations of prejudice since they recognize how detrimental it is for pupils. Nonetheless, with millions of teachers from diverse backgrounds and training, bigotry interferes in our schools as it does in the nation. Prejudice is a force in America. Its extent may be debatable; its existence is not.

Bigotry is hidden not only from those who are infected but also sometimes even from others who watch their actions. Rather than wearing a sign saying, "I am prejudiced," most people try to avoid giving any indication that they are infected. A destructive force is no less damaging because it is hidden.

An incident that was supposed to have happened in the life of playwright turned diplomat, Clare Booth Luce, was written up in press reports in 1954. Her biographers downplay the event, but it provides an analogy to illustrate the problems of prejudice. In 1954, President Eisenhower named Ms. Luce the American ambassador to Italy. Although she had been in good health when she began her duties, she became seriously ill after only a few months in her new position. Extensive testing discovered that she was being poisoned. Nobody could understand how or why. Investigators finally determined paint from the ceiling in the dining room of the old Italian villa she had leased was flaking in microscopic amounts and was dropping into her food as she ate. Over a period of time, the accumulation of these minute bits of toxic paint had sickened her. Hidden prejudice is an evil that poisons. Though it may be in tiny amounts and be hard to detect, it is lethal. Its disguised nature makes it difficult to discover and remove.

Prejudice has another powerful impact in schools: it is self-perpetuating because its casualties are those who are already behind. When a bigoted teacher subtly treats a weak student with disdain, the victim is pushed down even further. The possibility of success by the child becomes even more difficult. The instructor thereby sees an additional failure by this pupil and has another of

Terman's "facts" to justify, and perhaps increase, the existing prejudice. Another destructive negative cycle results: prejudice exists; prejudice increases the likelihood that the objects of prejudice will do poorly; poor performance then increases prejudice.

Unfortunately, another and still worse consequence follows: other students see this inferior progress. When pupils see that members of certain races do poorly in school, they have a tendency to believe they have found a "fact" about members of these races. Consequently, they will often carry negative ideas about that group with them into their outside lives. As adults, they may be prejudiced because of events in their early years, their school experiences. Under present conditions where poor scholarship is frequent in some races or nationalities, development of bigotry toward these groups is an inevitable result.

Any rational examination of the evils of prejudice shows that it must be eliminated, particularly in schools. Computerized education will reduce prejudice as no other system can. Since memories of computers are not influenced by what takes place around them, they have no prejudice, bias, or bigotry. Computers are unconcerned whether a student is black or white or Indian or Latino or Asian or a combination. They don't distinguish male students from female students. It is even irrelevant to computers whether a pupil is bright or dull. The machines, through their programming, merely adjust their teaching to meet the needs of the individual learner. Computers can teach each student at the student's own level without regard to any of the multiple concerns that could trigger prejudice in a human teacher.

Computerized education will eliminate bias and prejudice in teaching, but it will go further. It will destroy the basis of future prejudice among students who are influenced by seeing their fellow classmates of a particular type among the poorest students. This benefit will develop in two ways.

Those who are less adept at academic subjects will not stand out. Each student will be working at his or her own computer. Students will not compete and compare themselves against each other as frequently as today. They will be concentrating on their own learning. This will appreciably reduce derogatory comparisons with other groups of students. Pupils will work together in seminars and workshops, as I will show later, but they will be better able to do the work because they will not enter the cooperative projects until they are sufficiently prepared.

The more important way that computers will reduce future prejudice is by ensuring that all students can and will learn. As academic achievement improves for certain students, especially minority groups, the seeds of prejudice in the minds of other pupils will be lessened.

Computers, of course, cannot eliminate all prejudice. Bigoted instructors who have been influenced by their early learning will remain. With computerized education, however, attitudes of these teachers will be less damaging. I will show, in Chapter 19, how each student will have an individual Leader Teacher. Students will have only one teacher for at least a year at a time and will be able to choose whom they wish. They will be better able to select ones without prejudice toward them. The evil will be reduced because bigoted teachers will be less likely to deal with students who are objects of their prejudice.

Sexism

Bias or prejudice against different races, religions and patterns of ethnic customs is often glaring, but a more subtle form exists. It is directed against females, often in certain subjects such as mathematics and science.

Bias against women is sometimes considered to be an evil out of the murky past that has been eliminated. The American Association of University Women, however, put out a scathing report in February 1992.[49] This group had studied conditions confronting females in classrooms and concluded that hindrances to their scholastic success have not been eliminated or even begun to be addressed properly.

Before girls begin school, they test higher than boys. By the time they graduate from high school they are behind. Myra and David Sadker in their 1994 book *Failing at Fairness: How America's Schools Cheat Girls*, complain that, "Sitting in the same classroom, reading the same textbook, listening to the same teacher, boys and girls receive very different educations." In their extensive studies of schools these authors found repeated problems: girls are given less time to answer; boys are offered more detailed and constructive criticism; teachers interact with boys eight times more frequently than with girls; often when boys shout out an answer, it is accepted, but girls in the same class get reprimanded for that type of spontaneity. [50]

Many, perhaps most, teachers—even if they are unaware of their bias and deny it emphatically—are infected. Their negative attitudes may have begun when they, themselves, were students. Girls, subject to this discrimination may develop hesitations about their own talents. The result is prejudice directed at one's own sex that remains even when its causes have been long forgotten. This self-doubt may explain why females are often the first to say that they have no ability in math and science, although girls consistently get grades equal or better than boys do, in these subjects. This is probably an important reason why only 3 percent of science and engineering graduates are female. If they become teachers, they will in turn communicate these basic but hidden ideas to their students.

Boys, seeing the discrimination against girls, easily pick up the thought that males are superior in academics. Thereafter, they don't like to be equaled by females in subjects where they feel they are, or should be, better. Sometimes, they are so brazenly protective of their position that they intimidate girls into accepting it. Years later, as adults, the actions of these males may be unknowingly influenced by what they originally learned, or thought they learned, about females.

Girls, therefore, confront a huge hurdle in education. Massive numbers of instructors teach with some bias. Even under ideal conditions, changing teachers' attitudes toward women's abilities would take many years. Since most teachers don't know they are affected, simply telling them to change won't solve the plight of girls. Another answer is needed. Otherwise, sexist teaching will remain in schools. Many difficulties that girls face in classrooms can be addressed more easily by learning through computers than by any other means. Girls will have for the first time equal opportunity in all basic learning. Computerized education also will destroy a basis of future prejudice among students who might be influenced by seeing their female classmates belittled, however subtly, in today's classes.

Girls will be learning all their fundamentals through computers. Later, when their foundation is secure, they will join in cooperative projects with boys. The danger that females will again be demeaned in these cooperative undertakings will diminish appreciably. Girls will understand their own abilities and will have developed a basic confidence in their own talents.

Traditionalists may object that girls will feel uncomfortable with computers. That is a foolish objection, reminiscent of the ideas of earlier ages that girls should not go to school. Computers will intimidate neither girls nor boys; the machines will teach all children to feel at ease with this form of education.

All prejudice, whatever its form and against whomever it is directed, may be compared to cancer that eats away at the structure of the nation. Computerized education is essential in its eventual elimination in America.

Chapter 16
Eliminating Substitute Teachers

*A*n unfortunate practice in education today is the necessary use of substitute teachers. An instructor, absent from a class, must be replaced by someone who attempts to fill the void but with little knowledge of the class members and usually with less skill than the regular teacher. Alternatives don't exist.

The normal reaction of most people hearing about this condition is "Of course. What is unusual or detrimental about substitutes?" This type of reply epitomizes a frequent but woeful condition in education today. Educational tragedies are ignored because they have been around for many years, and people have grown accustomed to them. Having substitute teachers is an acute obstacle to improving education. The disorder is getting worse, yet it arouses little concern among parents or educators.

The number of classes requiring substitutes has been increasing sharply in recent years. The number of sick days allowed regular teachers has increased together with absences of teachers. This growth may be due simply to the additional days available but may result from the additional stress that teaching is placing on teachers, forcing them to require more days away from classrooms.

As the need expands, quality of substitutes decreases further from its already poor condition. Schools must grapple with the need to find sufficient numbers of temporary replacements. They are forced to lower their standards. Toch complains of:

> the lax credentialing standards that most states have for day-to-day substitutes. Only a handful of states require the same subject-matter background of secondary school substitutes as they

do of regular teachers, while many issue licenses that allow substitutes to teach any high school subject, and many more set no standards for substitute teachers at all. Of the states that do issue licenses to daily substitutes, half don't require a bachelor's degree, according to the [National Association of State Directors of Teacher Education and Certification] survey. Such standards are troublesome because teacher absenteeism is a tremendous problem in the public schools. It's not uncommon to find high schools with 10 percent, 15 percent, or even 20 percent of their teachers absent each day. As a result, thousands of the nation's public school classrooms are staffed by ill-trained substitutes daily.[1]

Even allowing for outstanding subs, the poor general quality is understandable. The problem starts with funding. Substitute teachers are paid less than regular teachers. This alone suggests that many subs will have poorer training and be less effective in classrooms than the permanent teacher.

Even if a specific substitute teacher happens to be talented and capable, effective teaching is not assured. Qualifications are only the beginning of the difficulties. A study of the history of the typical substitute teacher shows the genesis of problems. Subs sign up with a central office in the school system. They must provide a record of their credits and teaching endorsements. A potential substitute with good qualifications in one subject may be allowed to go on the list for many more subjects that are only remotely related. School systems need substitutes and want as many subs as they can corral to be on their list. The system loses nothing if a sub is never used in a school. If, however, the day comes when a substitute is unavailable, the principal suddenly confronts a formidable problem. Classes must be covered, and almost any living, breathing body may be acceptable if no one else is available. No class can be left unattended.

This signing-up process usually ends the substitute's preparatory work toward becoming a sub. Some morning at the bright and cheerful hour of 6:00 AM, the phone rings and rouses the sub from what we hope was a sound sleep because he or she will need the strength that comes from a restful night. The necessary information is communicated to the substitute: the school, its location, and the subjects for which the permanent teacher is responsible. The day's saga for the

temporary instructor and the thirty members in each of his or her classes is about
to begin. Frequently, it is a true adventure for both teacher and students.

The substitute hopes to find a lesson plan for that day, prepared by the
regular teacher. Under ideal circumstances, the permanent teacher has provided a detailed plan. This sometimes happens, but often it does not. On
occasion, the teacher not only fails to leave a suitable lesson plan but also may
leave only the barest outline, and occasionally, no lesson plan. Regular teachers
often feel that the sub will accomplish little and that they will have to repeat the
lesson. Under these conditions, teachers have little incentive to spend a lot of
extra effort trying to make sure that a detailed lesson plan is prepared. Motivation for the teacher to prepare the students for the sub is also lacking. Regular
faculty members often refer to substitutes as "expensive baby-sitters."

Sometimes regular teachers know that they will be gone, as, for example,
when they are going to a conference. When that occurs, teachers are more likely
to leave detailed instructions for the substitute. Often, of course, a teacher
awakes feeling ill at 5:30 AM, and the principal's office must arrange for a sub at
6:00 AM. Without a detailed lesson plan, the substitute teacher enters that class
at an intimidating disadvantage.

The biggest problem confronting substitute teachers is the attitude of
class members. The students know that their relationship with this instructor is
temporary, and this interloper will have nothing to do with final grading. The
substitute is unfamiliar with the class and unaware of which students may cause
difficulties. Even skilled substitute teachers find this a difficult predicament.
One teacher, whom I know, did some subbing while she worked on an advanced
degree in another town. She is an excellent teacher and never had a difficulty
with discipline when she taught full time. Nonetheless, she said she wasted an
undue amount of her time establishing discipline in classes where she was a
sub. She described her experiences that year as providing students with a "license to raise hell."

Frequently, the classes that require many substitutes are those that have
the poorest discipline even while the regular teacher is present. Teachers are
human and suffer normal psychological stress. Those who have classes with
unruly students will find teaching agonizingly difficult. They will often be the

ones who need frequent relief from the rigors of the classroom. A substitute going into a class that is accustomed to poor discipline with the regular teacher will find conditions that day to be horrendous. Even when regular teachers have a disciplined class, subs must still struggle to maintain that condition.

If substitutes are those who are less qualified or are taking on classes for which they are poorly trained, students will spot the deficiencies quickly. A few students will understand and pounce on any indications of teacher weakness. The day's contest begins to unfold, and the students have the position of strength.

This reliance on subs creates an immediate and obvious difficulty. About 8 percent of teachers across the nation are absent on any given day. Thus, almost one school day in twelve may be less than ideal. Considering this, how can anyone, who seriously considers the stress that use of substitutes inflicts on education, airily dismiss the practice?

The problem is not new, only worsening. Substitute teachers have meant poorer education for students for many years. A study was done in New York schools in 1974. The findings were conclusive and showed that substitute teachers were significantly less effective in teaching than regular teachers.[2]

Many educators understand these problems. They write articles in educational journals suggesting means of improving substitute teaching.[3] Making substantial changes is challenging, however, because of many inherent problems. A major one is the high turnover rate among substitutes. Subbing is an unpleasant job and pays poorly. Why would a sub continue if he or she could find another job? Many articles on improving the lot of substitute teachers advocate more training by school systems, but if schools develop an elaborate system for improving individual subs, the effort is wasted when the substitute leaves.

The practice is absolutely unchangeable in the present system of education in which instruction is totally dependent upon an individual teacher who has full responsibility for supervising learning of a specific subject. In computerized education, there will be no substitute teachers since the computer will be teaching. A human monitor will be required in most classrooms but without needing to be knowledgeable in any particular subject. Monitors will assist, encourage, and support students but will not provide academic material. Professional teachers will sometimes be monitors. It will give them additional opportunities to interact with the students. Often, however, monitoring will be done by paraprofessionals, equivalent to today's "teacher's aides." When a regular monitor is absent, others on staff, either teachers or paraprofessionals, will be able to step into that position.

Wiping out the involvement of substitute teachers will by itself bring massive benefits to education. Up to one day in twelve will no longer be wasted.

Chapter 17

Added Gains

Computerized education will provide other peripheral benefits, and their cumulative value is considerable.

Students will not be penalized by ordinary absences. Most students miss days during their schooling because of illness. At least inconvenience, if not more severe difficulties, hinders students when they return and try to catch up. In the computer schools, lessons will always begin where the previous one ended, regardless of the time lag. Vacations will not have to be predetermined and taken by everybody simultaneously. Whenever a parent wishes to remove a student from class to travel with the family, the student will fit in exactly when the trip is completed. Workshops, seminars, and field trips, which will be vital in computerized education, can be scheduled without concern about missing classes.

Children will not be required to wait for an arbitrary date to start their schooling. Under today's system, children cannot begin their formal education whenever they reach a specified birthday but must wait until the next time the school system can begin a new class, usually about the beginning of September. Just as children will be able to have vacations at any time, they will be able to begin at any time.

The need for records and paperwork with the accompanying possibility of errors will be less burdensome to school systems. Paperwork will be drastically reduced. Computers will develop and keep necessary records and print them or transmit them instantaneously and accurately to other files when needed.

Teaching will not be bound by current time constraints. Computers are tireless and can work and instruct at anytime and under virtually any circumstances. They are not limited to an eight-hour day or forty-hour week. They don't need vacations and are never hampered by physical illness or psychological problems. Burnout for a computer can be remedied by simply replacing either a part of the machine or the whole computer.

Time spent learning in school can be increased. Students in the United States attend school about 180 days each year. Other countries including Germany, Japan, and England have many more days in their school calendar—up to 240 days in some industrialized nations. This time differential is piled atop the other shortcomings in American education, but no solution is available under present conditions. To extend schooling today would require tens of thousands of additional teachers. Schools are unable to find them especially in the critical areas of math and science. Even if they could be located, they could not be employed. School budgets that have trouble supporting present expenditures could not find the added revenue needed to increase schooling by 33 percent. Although the additional learning that will follow from computerized education may obviate the necessity of extending the school year, schools will be able to provide the additional schooling. The machines will be available with little additional cost. Moreover, increased time could be provided in diverse ways. Schools could be open on Saturday or Sunday for some students, while others continue a Monday-to-Friday schedule. Classes could be available twelve months a year, and students and their parents could decide when to attend. Computers would easily track attendance and ensure it met school requirements.

Computerized education will always be current. As information in the world explodes, teachers find it difficult to keep up with all developments. Keeping students abreast of new advances is particularly important in scientific fields. It is much easier to update one computer program that will be used in thousands of classrooms than to update the working knowledge of thousands of teachers now in those classrooms.

Important additions to learning that are now overlooked in most schools can be added easily. Every student will learn to type soon after learning to read. Pupils will acquire a skill that will remain with them for the remainder of their lives and provide many benefits. Another important addition that will be universally included will be instruction in reading faster with improved comprehension. Speed reading courses have often been available outside formal education for fees, but few schools devote much time to cultivating this talent. This omission may be due to the lack of training of teachers or to the wide diversity of reading skills within a class. Computers have neither limitation and are ideally suited to develop faster reading because they can easily increase or decrease the rate that words appear on the monitor. The machines will test understanding immediately and develop the students' facility with printed text. Rapid reading with high comprehension is a skill that can be learned and will be a basic competency that students develop early, improve periodically, and retain throughout their lives.

Computers used by students during the day will be available in the evening for ongoing adult education programs. Lifetime learning fulfills a basic desire and is popular in many retirement communities. *AMERICA 2000* encouraged this movement stating: "The president is urging every American to continue learning throughout his or her life." This document asked Americans to become a "nation of students." This lofty goal is difficult to attain because increased learning is usually dependent on instructors who are costly. Computerized education will be as valuable for older students as for younger ones. Programming can be developed that will instruct the learners about use of the machines and use of other software, without the need for human teachers.

Many other parts of society will profit. Taxpayers will gain because the cost of education will be reduced. Business will benefit since the work force will be better educated and will not require remedial education. School administrators will rejoice when they have fewer discipline problems. Since crime and illiteracy are intimately connected, a literate society will lessen lawlessness to the benefit of all, but especially to law enforcement officials. The nation as a whole will benefit from computerized education because its citizens will be better prepared to compete in the global economy that envelops the world today.

Teachers will benefit since they will find more personal satisfaction in their profession. Their work will be more exciting, challenging, and enjoyable. They will see more accomplishments from their efforts. Moreover, they should be better paid since their jobs will be even more important. The new role of teachers will be covered more extensively in the following chapters.

Parents, of course, will take great delight in knowing that their children are well educated. Students, however, will be the foremost beneficiaries of computerized education exactly as they are the ones who suffer most from the educational debacle of today. Their gains are recounted throughout this book.

NEW
TEACHERS
AND
SCHOOLS

Chapter 18

General Activities of Future Teachers

Whil computers appeared in a form and price that made them widely available, some parents and educators shuddered. They feared that authorities under the guise of "progress" could foist machines on students and employ these lifeless but adept mechanical monsters to tamper with the minds of children. They anguished that these new instruments could bring a mechanistic world where machines dominated learning, and students became more like automatons than humans. They cringed at the vision of a school system where technology would jettison human teachers and make education mechanical and impersonal.

These nightmares may have contributed to the sluggish employment of the full power of computers in schools. Fortunately, however, these wild fears are totally wrong. Computerized education will not bring a harsh, unfeeling school system because teachers will prevent that catastrophe. They will remain in schools, and they will provide a uniquely human element as machines provide the vast stores of knowledge. They will ensure that education forms and develops the whole person, not merely the intellectual side.

The role of teachers, however, must change. When computers are fully used in schools, human instructors will no longer have a grade or a class assigned to them. They will not relay academic information to students by lecturing, assigning readings, showing films or audiovisual displays, or by using computers to assist their teaching. They will no longer be forced to make daily lesson plans and the routine preparations for classes. They won't have to devise and correct tests. Their paperwork will almost be eliminated. It will not be their responsibility to cover a specific section of the curriculum over a given time. They won't be obligated to produce marks, nor make the painful decision whether to pass or fail a borderline student.

Elimination of these traditional duties will enable them to perform other crucial tasks that only a human can carry out. Feeling, sensitive, human teachers will be better able to develop feeling, sensitive, human students. Long ago Plato said, "The direction in which education starts a man will determine his future life."[1] Computers will give teachers greater freedom to provide that necessary direction. The greatest personal benefit for teachers will be the success they achieve in educating their pupils. Everything detailed in Chapter 12 about the need to succeed applies equally to teachers. Their success is dependent upon the success of their students. If their pupils fail to learn, they also suffer. One teacher in the Florida at-risk program pointed out this discouraging side of teaching to me. She said she always felt she was an excellent teacher, but she had been frustrated by her classroom results before beginning in the computer program. When students are unable to progress, the agony and feeling of hopelessness is found not only in the pupils; their instructors share the pain.

Just as students are held back by the restrictions placed on them by present schools, teachers are also under harsh constraints. Not only must they try to teach the same material simultaneously to twenty or thirty students, but they must also contend with unending activities, many only peripheral to student learning. They are like jugglers who must expend their limited energy keeping everything going and have little time to concentrate on any individual object. They must forego precious opportunities to help students reach their full potential. Thomas Edison's mother came to an appreciation of the brilliance of her pupil through her continual interaction with him. With that knowledge, she was able start him on the path that altered the history of the world.

Despite many external differences, however, the primary mission of teachers will be unchanged: they will continue to be educators. They will fulfill their true vocation of leading children out of ignorance, and they will do it more effectively. Computers will provide the huge quantity of information now available for students to absorb, but teachers will continually encourage them to integrate this learning into their lives and will show them how to do it. They will ease the difficulties that the explosion of knowledge will impose on children trying to keep up in an information-based world. They will help pupils harmonize the data absorbed from computers into their value systems. They will encourage and stimulate students to obtain a full education. They will smooth the challenges of interpersonal development among youths and will make it easier for them to mature.

Society has always esteemed great teachers. This high regard will continue and increase. Many characteristics of teachers that predominate in computerized education will be the same as those that the best instructors have always had and for which their former students remember them. When adults comment about the teachers who influenced their lives, they recount many meaningful traits. They remember a teacher's ability to inspire them to excel and to show them how to do it. They praise the ability of an instructor who taught them to appreciate a particular subject and stimulated them to seek additional learning. They recall an inspiring human who gave them encouragement when matters looked difficult or who brought out their latent and unknown abilities. Some look back with gratitude toward a teacher who helped them pass through the trying years of youth and to enter better-prepared into adulthood. In computer schools, these same abilities will continue to enhance the lives of students, and teachers will be better positioned for their important responsibilities.

While computers use their unique power to instruct and enlighten, teachers will use their humanness to educate and uplift. They will ensure a distinctly human element in education while allowing computers to convey information, a task for which the machines are singularly equipped. Computers will instruct; teachers will educate.

Obstacles

Serious change never happens easily. Certain teachers may fear to relinquish many of their present duties to which they have grown accustomed. These instructors may hesitate or even fight this new program and may suggest a compromise: let teachers remain in their present role but let additional computers be purchased so that children will have more opportunity to interact with the machines while remaining in the familiar classroom situation.

I hope I have shown by now that this "compromise" cannot be successful. Computers—millions of them—have not changed education in the present arrangement. Millions more won't change education either, unless the system is fundamentally different. If teachers continue to control the flow of information in the usual way, they will block the power of computers, and they, themselves, will remain locked in the present inadequate system. Only when computers provide information to students without being subject to the training, skills, and personality of individual teachers can education truly change. Only when computers relieve teachers of the time consuming myriad of their present tasks can these human mentors reach their maximum productivity.

Unquestionably, for some teachers the change will not be easy. For these, their difficulties can and must be eased by the administration. They will need encouragement and will require additional training. This will be a small price for schools to pay for the eventual massive gains they will garner from the more efficient use of teachers and computers.

Many of today's teachers, however, will find their shift to this new world of education easy and natural. They will immediately realize that many creative approaches, which they wanted to use but had been unable to handle in the past, will now be open to them. The joy that they now experience from educating children will be enhanced.

Chapter 19

Specific Activities of Future Teachers

*I*t is now time to become more explicit and to detail ways by which teachers will use their additional time to become better educators. I will take two chapters for this explanation. This first will present the basic ideas, and Chapter 20 will follow one teacher for one day. An important caveat must be included: it is impossible to visualize precisely what the future will hold because innovative teachers will use their new found time to devise ways to enrich students that we can't imagine today.

Leader Teachers

Of all the changes that will flow from computerized education, perhaps the most visible will be the new relationships that will develop between teachers and students. Each student will always have one instructor who will have personal responsibility over a period of time for assisting that child to learn and grow and progress. I call this person the Leader Teacher. As a result of Leader Teachers, no student will pass through school without individual attention throughout his or her scholastic career. This is radically different from today when some students do not meet with a teacher for a personal conference for months or even years.

Leader Teachers will have access to all scholastic records of their individual students. The computer will provide information about every subject, and instructors will know if their pupils are progressing, or are deficient according to norms for finishing school by an approximate age. In turn, students will always be aware if they are advancing at a sufficiently fast pace. The first objective of their teachers will be to ensure that they are on track to reach the basic goals.

Leader Teachers will meet with their students for individual discussion as often as is helpful. For some students that will be more frequent than for others depending on their age, status, and individual needs. These sessions will help bring the child's education to fruition. In addition to directing the student, teachers will be able to add a human element to the continual encouragement that computers will be giving to pupils. They will be able honestly to build upon and enhance the success that pupils will attain as shown in Chapter 12. They will encourage students to go beyond the basic educational requirements and to delve into other areas that might prove interesting, or to go much deeper into intriguing subjects.

This book has emphasized the rewards that students will reap because computers will serve them as private tutors to instruct them individually. I believe another important gain will accrue to pupils because they will have private teachers to direct them individually. In computerized education, teachers will know students better and direct them, not as members of a class of thirty but as an individual person. Students will harvest phenomenal gains from this personal attention, while teachers who chose their profession because they wished to help students to become educated, will find their activities rewarding and satisfying.

Students, together with their parents, will choose their Leader Teachers, who will then direct the pupils over the course of at least a year but often for several years. This arrangement of having a specific assigned teacher will be somewhat analogous to a doctoral candidate in a university who has a faculty member responsible for directing him or her through the pitfalls of writing a dissertation. Leader Teachers will shepherd their students through the pitfalls of achieving an education. The supervision necessary will vary with age and ability. While students are least mature, teachers will provide the most intense direction. As the children advance, they will assume more self-direction, but they will always meet regularly with their Leaders.

Difficulties of students that are not scholastic may be addressed by the teachers themselves, or by counselors in consultation with the teacher. Normal discipline problems will be first relayed to the Leader Teacher. For example, the computer will track absences and immediately notify the Teacher. If a student is disruptive in a class, the monitor will note it on the student's record, and the main computer will make this known to the Leader Teacher immediately. When a discipline problem is beyond the capability of a Teacher, the child will be referred to the proper authorities.

Leader Teachers will meet with their students individually but also in groups. These meetings will not be like today's ordinary classes but will aim to have students interact and to discuss topics of interest under the direction of their Teacher. Specific times will be allotted to the meeting of students who have the same Leader. Depending on circumstances including the number of students whom a Teacher is directing, all or only some students may participate each time.

While teachers will be a resource for students for help in deciding the direction they should go and the optional courses they should take, no one can be qualified or knowledgeable in every subject. Students may, at times, need information on a subject outside their Leader Teacher's field. Another instructor with that expertise will be made available to the student for a conference on the recommendation of his or her own Leader Teacher.

Leader Teachers and Parents

Whatever the underlying strength of schools, additional encouragement and direction from parents will always provide extremely valuable assistance in the education of their children. Therefore, involving parents will remain a high priority of schools. The Leader Teacher will be the one whom parents contact.

This will have an immediate benefit: parents will need to meet with only one teacher who will have information on all the child's classes and activities. Whenever parent-teacher conferences occur, instructors will easily be able to provide complete and up-to-the-minute information on the child's progress through the computer records and through their own intimate contact with the student. Teachers will provide not only verbal reports but also graphic computer print outs that will explain clearly how the child is moving toward the goal of obtaining an education. The machine will provide additional information about possible future educational objectives based on the current status of the child.

The additional time available to teachers will make it easier for parents to arrange conferences that will fit in with their own sometimes-hectic schedules. Moreover, the bonds between teacher and parents (as between teacher and student) will be stronger, especially if they and the child choose to retain the same Leader Teacher for several years. This stronger bond will, in turn, encourage greater parental involvement.

Despite the undeniable value of having parents participate in the education of their children, many parents will forego or minimize this activity. Computerized education can partially compensate for this inescapable condition better than present schools. Often the child whose parents do not become involved with the school is the one for whom guidance at home is also deficient. A teacher can never assume the position of the parent, but a concerned instructor can provide an important supplement and be a role model. For the sake of children and of society, youths must be directed during their formative years. Where the parent does not do it, someone else may be able to help. Excellent teachers have always done this, and they will be able to expand their efforts in the future.

Conducting Seminars and Workshops

Beyond their role as Leaders, teachers will have other interaction with the children. These additional duties will also be ones that only a human educator can fulfill. Devising and carrying out seminars, workshops, debates, and other cooperative and interactive projects will be prominent duties of teachers. In these activities, teachers will again enhance and extend education beyond the limits of computer competency.

Teachers will spend a substantial portion of their time on these undertakings. Most teachers will be expected to develop projects in their field of academic training. These activities will not be limited only to a narrow section of work defined by a curriculum since all necessary fundamentals will be taught to students by computers. As teachers plan and develop their workshops, there will be few limits on their imagination. They will be able to lead small groups of students into new and perhaps at times, uncharted areas, where creativity of both teacher and students can flourish. Instructors will encourage students to develop advanced habits of thinking and analysis while teaching pupils to work together. Seminars and workshops will provide important opportunities for discussions among students and will help them learn to work together.

Teachers are accustomed to initiate interactive student learning in classrooms today. They will continue these familiar patterns while conducting seminars and workshops. In computerized education, their success will be magnified because they will have more time to prepare for these activities and ideal conditions to carry them out. Students will also be better prepared and will have better attitudes because they will be participating in something they choose to do.

Additionally, students will have a certain freedom in making their choices of groups in which they wish to participate. Since various topics will be available, they will be able to delve into subjects that intrigue them. Most of the seminars or workshops that they attend will not be with their own Leader Teacher, but their participation will always require the approval of their personal mentors who will know them and their abilities intimately. The immaturity of the student that might result in poor selection will be tempered by the experience of the Leader Teacher.

Allowing pupils to select their seminars will give them an opportunity to take an active part in setting up their educational program. On the other side, giving students the right to choose seminars in which they wish to participate may frighten some teachers when they first think about the possibility. Until now, they have had an audience that was required to attend, and usually they weren't concerned about filling their classes. When students can choose to take or pass up workshops or seminars, a new element will appear in education.

Some teachers may find the transition to a student choice arrangement difficult without additional help from authorities. It should be made available to them exactly as other advanced learning is provided today. Teachers, however, will not be judged on numbers of attendees they attract. For example, only a few students will be interested and have the ability needed to analyze characters in Shakespearean tragedies. Teachers conducting these seminars cannot be considered as less able if only a few students sign up. Courses of this caliber probably will be held with students from several schools able to participate.

Since teachers will establish requirements for entry into workshops, students will be prepared when they attend. The interaction of well-prepared students with similar interests under the direction of an enthusiastic teacher will provide conditions for optimal learning. Teachers will spark and foster this interplay. They will prod students to think deeply. They will also provide a valuable and professional opinion on subjects under discussion, but bright, motivated participants will often come to their own conclusions. These students will be advancing in self-directed learning that will have had its beginning on the first day in kindergarten.

All these group activities will be ungraded, but only students will be allowed to attend who have fulfilled the prerequisites and are willing to make the efforts needed to be prepared. The teacher or teachers who direct the seminar will assign multimedia presentations to be viewed together with readings both from books and from the Internet. That will encourage adequate preparation to ensure that students are ready and qualified to take part in discussions.

Since individual striving for grades will not interfere with group effort, cooperative work toward a common goal will be fostered more easily. The push of competition might still be employed with one class competing against another class in another school. Students working together in a common struggle will allow both cooperation and competition. Telecommunications will make this possible.

Critics might question whether students will do more than go through the formalities of attending seminars without grades to motivate them. In reality, powerful precedents already exist for students taking courses without getting grades or credit. School systems often conduct summer sessions and attract students with unusual courses that don't carry credits. Many learning camps require pupils to pay to attend although the courses are without credit. Learning also takes place in many extracurricular activities that consume time of students but with no consideration of school credits.

Merely because only a few students in today's schools would take non-credit seminars means nothing. The current educational system often deprives students of the necessary enjoyment. In the Florida at-risk programs, learning is stimulating and intrigues students who had been completely disdainful of schooling before their computerized education.

Although some students may shirk their responsibilities in ungraded seminars, they will still be much better educated through computerized education than in today's schools. Teachers will have the time to make seminars interesting, and that will entice students to take them and work in them. Peer pressure will also be a valuable force. Schools will be smaller as will be seen in Chapter 21. Peer pressure has many negative effects today, but in smaller schools it will be a positive force. Students will find education in enjoyable seminars to be stimulating. Today's frequent condition where students are apathetic in gigantic impersonal institutions will no longer be a factor in education.

Other Considerations

Although computers are powerful teachers, they have obvious limits to what they can achieve. For example, computers can't judge creativity since they only carry out what has been included in their programming. Anything truly creative is therefore new, and consequently, is outside the scope of what they can have in their memories. This restriction may change sometime when work on artificial intelligence achieves greater results. In the foreseeable future, however, and probably always, judgment of creativity will be restricted to humans.

Advanced fiction writing is an area that is dependent upon creativity. All students will learn to write a decent paper with proper use of grammar and sentence construction. Computer programs now exist that can teach and evaluate basic writing skills, and these, like all software, will continually improve. Any student, however, who wishes to go further in writing, will need other options. Creative writing seminars will be an important possibility. Some students may want to start magazines in their fields although they will have limited circulation or may be available only on the Internet.

Besides writing, many other areas of learning could be enhanced by development of creativity. For example, finding possible solutions for any of the myriad of crises in the nation and around the world could prod students to devise and justify new approaches. Teachers will be responsible for encouraging innovation in their seminars and workshops. They will have more time to help students formulate and then elaborate new ideas because workshops will extend over a full day, or over several days, or perhaps may occur periodically throughout a lengthier period.

An added benefit for students, but also for teachers, will be interchange of ideas from students and teachers in other schools. Certain participants in advanced seminars will make their work available for criticism through the Internet. In turn, they will evaluate student work from other locations. These will be learning experiences both for the student doing the review and for the one being judged.

The self-directed element combined with seminars and workshops, and teachers directing this learning will have similarities with what takes place in better graduate schools today. This emulation is desirable because American graduate schools provide some of the foremost examples of outstanding education anywhere in the world. Their value entices many foreign students to come to the United States for advanced studies.

Exercising Their Initiative

Teachers will find the potential of computerized education and their position in it to be exhilarating. They will find new outlets for their initiative and ingenuity, and the educational system will be enhanced even further. Although education, both in and outside the classroom, advances today through their creativity, they are still restricted and often stymied in their attempts. When they are able to use their talents more fully, both they and their students will benefit.

An example of the abilities of teachers aiding education beyond simple teaching is in a movement known as "empowerment." The basic idea is that teachers assume more responsibility for schooling by being "empowered" by authorities to make many decisions that higher authorities formerly imposed upon them. A continuing difficulty is that teachers must grapple with these new responsibilities without any additional time. Nonetheless, empowerment has shown laudable results. Teachers, freed from many present burdens, will be able to give the movement a valid test.

The individuality of teachers will be retained, and they will never be carbon copies of each other. Even in the duties they choose, their different skills and talents will be stressed. For example, some instructors may be better as Leader Teachers and others may be exceptionally well qualified to conduct advanced learning seminars and workshops.

In computerized education, students will be the primary beneficiaries, but teachers will share in the rewards. When instructors are relieved of tedious routine work, they will be better able to educate youth, the reason they became teachers. These new opportunities will likely attract more of the brightest young people into education as their life's work.

Computers will never eliminate human pedagogy. They will make the profession more satisfying, engaging, and fulfilling. They will allow teachers to be better educators, the ultimate reward for any dedicated instructor.

Chapter 20

October 19, 2010

*T*he workday of different teachers in computerized education will vary widely just as do the schedules of today's instructors. Nonetheless, we can come to a feel for the pattern of teachers in that era if we look at one day in the life of one teacher. We'll choose Mary Johnson, who has a degree in English literature. We'll look at her activities on October 19, 2010. Mary is the Leader Teacher for students who range in age from eleven to fifteen

When Ms. Johnson comes to school at 8:30 AM on that day, she goes immediately to her "office" that is small and simple but is hers alone. In her room she has two chairs, her computer station, and storage shelves holding her books and the successors to today's computer disks and CD-ROMS. Her walls are decorated with a couple of pictures that she likes and has brought from her home because they add a warm touch to her surroundings.

On the morning we are watching her, she begins, as she begins everyday, by signing on to her computer and connecting to the main computer of the school. From there she receives the list of activities she has previously scheduled for today. On any given day, these might include a class that she will oversee, a group meeting that she has set up with all or some of the students for whom she is the Leader Teacher, a seminar that she is conducting, individual conferences with her students or parents that she has previously arranged, or a meeting with the other teachers to discuss many decisions that must be made by the school such as allocation of the funding that the government provides to the school.

Her computer will check to see if any student for whom she is the Leader Teacher has left her a note requesting to see her today. If there is such a message, that will take priority, and she will immediately allocate time on her schedule for that meeting. She will leave her reply on the main computer giving the student a time to come to her office. Her student will see the message as soon as he or she logs on for the day. Notice of that meeting will go into the record of that pupil. After the conference is completed she will add a note about what took place.

Mary is the Leader Teacher for thirty students. This is about average across the nation although some have more, some less, depending on many factors such as the age of students and their difficulties, and the preferences of teachers themselves about expending their time.

Mary's pupils look to her as their friend, guide, and primary resource. She has been in this role for five of her students for three years; the rest have been with her for either one or two years, except for the six that are with her for the first time this year. Each day the computer will check the records of all thirty of her students to see if any are having obvious problems with keeping up, with attendance, with discipline, or with any other problem. If the computer finds anything that may be the least bit askew in the record of any of her pupils, Ms. Johnson will be informed. If she concurs that something may be wrong, she will probably schedule a meeting with that student also for today.

Next she will see the list of all of her pupils and the time that they last had a personal conference with her. She may at that time schedule meetings with some of them for a couple of days later. Notification to the students will appear on their computers when they next sign in.

Mary will then check her phone and E-mail messages. These might be from a parent wishing to arrange a meeting with her, or from the school authorities giving her information to relay to her students during their next group meeting. There may be a message from a fellow teacher or from someone on the Internet to whom she had sent a question previously.

Mary's schedule is now fairly well set for the day. She has a group session with the older sixteen of her thirty students from 9:00 to 9:45. At this group meeting, she has a couple of announcements about routine matters that were first brought to the students' attention in messages from the principal's office to their computers. Mary's main objective of this meeting, however, is to generate discussion about the election that will take place in November. She will have some of the students take the Republican candidates and some the Democratic for a debate on the Monday before Election Day. It will be up to the students today to lay down the ground rules for this debate including the offices to be covered and how to find the opinions of the candidates on the important issues.

She is to monitor a class today from 10:00 to 11:00. She enjoys these monitoring sessions because she sees exactly how students interact with computers and with their fellow students.

She found when she checked at the beginning of the day that one of her students asked to see her today. She will see him from 11:30 to 12:00 after she has called all his records and looked them over. He didn't give any indication of what he wanted the conference for, but she does know that he has been considering adding extra time on history since he enjoys the subject. Ms. Johnson is probably going to suggest a weeklong seminar on the World War I era about which she has just been informed. It will be held at another school early next year.

She will see two other students after lunch. These are regular sessions that she usually has about every week to three weeks with her pupils. She will have all their records and will discuss how they are getting along and where they are going. One of the pupils comes from a family with only one parent. The mother died last year, and this pupil, a girl, is struggling with the death and needs a lot of attention. Mary always sees this pupil every few days. The other, also a girl, is at the opposite end of the spectrum. This youngster delights in school, has great deal of support and encouragement from her parents, and does not need as much day to day attention. This is one of the students who have had Mary as Leader for three years. The girl chose her primarily because she likes literature and Mary has been able to encourage and foster that liking. Although she only sees this student about once every three weeks (except when the student attends one of Mary's seminars) the computer brings up her record regularly and Ms. Johnson knows the girl is continuing to progress. She will spend time today simply encouraging her and trying to stimulate her to do more creative writing and to submit pieces to several of the varied publications that are springing up in schools across the city. Mary has toyed with the idea of urging some students that she knows to start one of these publications, but she feels she needs additional training on the basic idea before getting the students involved. She has applied to attend a statewide conference on this subject in March.

When these conferences with the students are finished today, Mary will enter something about each meeting in the pupil's computer record, which she will again see before their next session. All her notes are always available to her through her password anytime she calls the child's records. The rest of the afternoon she will devote to preparing for the seminar on Elizabethan England that she is scheduled to hold from 9:00 to 3:30 on November 17th, 18th, and 19th. Three of the participants will be students for whom she is the Leader Teacher, and attendance of eight other pupils, including four from other schools, has been approved by their own Leader Teachers.

Mary wants to put out her preparatory list of materials today. She knows that there is a new material available that she believes might give additional background information. She will spend time this afternoon checking on that. If that disk has what she expects, she will notify all eleven participating students that it is being held for them in the library and she will spell out the sections that she wants them to read before the seminar. The manufacturer of that particular disk allows material to be downloaded to the computers of pupils at school without infringing on the copyright, since the company feels it is good advertising. Mary will also give the attendees a list of other materials, including several sites on the Internet that she expects them to preview before November 17th. She will send this message to their computer box numbers, and they will all see the message sometime today before they leave school. Students from other schools will be notified by E-mail, and they will be expected to respond telling her they have received her message. If any of the pupils from her school is absent today, Mary will be informed and will be told when the pupil returns and receives the lists.

Mary will spend considerable time making her preparations for the seminar over the next few days. One objective she has already determined will be to have the students consider how the various authors in that time frame influenced each other. Since these attendees are particularly bright, this will probably stimulate them to jump into the controversy that periodically erupts about who actually wrote the plays of Shakespeare. She, of course, has her opinion, but she will keep that to herself. It is always intriguing with a group of outstanding students who obviously have an interest in that era (or they wouldn't be taking the seminar) to see what ideas they will develop.

Finally, Mary will have one more important activity for today. She has a parent conference at 5:30. That will take about an hour while she goes through all the records of the student, and she and the parents and the student discuss what his future course of studies should be.

When 6:30 comes, Mary will have put in a lengthy day. She is planning on taking Friday off because she and her husband have a long weekend planned and the extra hours today will cover part of that day off. She has already accumulated several hours with other parent conferences during the past few weeks.

When Mary finally does leave school she has one advantage that earlier teachers could only dream about: her work is finished. There are no tests to correct, no lesson plans to make for tomorrow, no grades to develop. She is free to rest to be ready to give her students her undivided attention tomorrow, Wednesday, October 20, 2010.

Chapter 21

Future Schools

*T*hat imposing figure in American education, James Bryant Conant, was mentioned in Chapter 1. His tenure as president of Harvard University gave him credibility in the teaching community and made his suggestions readily acceptable. Nothing was done about his accurate prediction of impending turmoil in the inner cities, probably because no one knew what to do.

One suggestion of his that was embraced and followed was about the size of schools. In the late 1950s he headed a group of educators and researchers who studied many facets of schooling. They completed what appeared to be a thorough evaluation of the condition of secondary education. Their conclusions of that study were issued in a short book in 1959. They advanced several recommendations, but one idea predominated. Conant authored the book covering their ideas and he wrote:

> The number of small high schools must be drastically reduced
> .... Aside from this important change, I believe no radical alteration
> in the basic pattern of American education is necessary to improve
> our public high schools.[1]

The reasoning of Conant about school size was based on a simple principle: larger schools can offer better education because a small school is unable to hire instructors with the education needed to teach advanced classes if only one or two students would take them. Without these teachers, small schools must forego offering superior courses in math, science, social studies, and languages. A large school, however, can provide these highly skilled instructors because many students will want these opportunities. Eliminating small schools, therefore, would improve education. Larger schools should also be less expensive to operate because of savings of volume. For example, only one cafeteria is required in a large school instead of three in three smaller schools.

Conant's strong recommendations ushered in a new era in school building. The influence of his credentials drove the switch to larger institutions, and the movement quickly gained momentum. Small schools became passé. "Bigger is better" became a cliché in education. The recommendations were dutifully followed by school districts across America. Conant's wishes were fulfilled. The number of small schools was sharply reduced. Enormous schools, especially in metropolitan areas flourished. Conant had started a major movement.

As proponents of bigness gained adherents and school boards fell in line, extensive research attempted to substantiate the theoretical value of the larger institutions. The results were not conclusive but indicated that the original ideas about better education and monetary savings probably were valid.[2]

That early research, however, had a flaw: it overlooked the psychological well being of students. When later studies looked at the mental health of students in large schools, the results were quite different. Better teachers provided better education for some students, but many students suffered in the massive institutions.

Small schools make many contributions to student well being. For example, pupils in small schools participate more in extra curricular activities and are less alienated than students in large schools.[3] Other benefits of smaller schools also are important to the mental health of children: closer staff-pupil relationships aid students, and smaller schools are "more conducive to participating, emotionally healthy student populations."[4]

One group that never fully accepted the principle that "bigger is better" were the mothers and fathers of students. They couldn't get their wishes recognized while the juggernaut rolled on. Nonetheless, parents continued to prefer smaller schools. Reduced size brings more neighborhood locations, allowing greater interchange among guardians because they are more likely to know each other. Smaller schools also promote better communication between school staff and parents.

A study of schools in Montgomery County in Maryland gave other possible reasons why smaller schools are better. In that district smaller schools were found to have teachers who were more innovative, and their staffs took on administrative responsibilities more readily and had a voice in running the school. They were credited with a family atmosphere in which children, teachers, and parents could know each other and create a supportive environment, while developing close community relationships. These smaller schools tended to have a principal who knew staff members better and could make the best use of them.[5]

Even the supposed diminished costs in larger schools began to be questioned because of the expense of busing. When more students enroll in a school, the average commute of students must increase, requiring more extensive transportation. Advocates of large schools had often ignored this factor when they estimated savings.

Unfortunately, it was only after jumbo schools were well entrenched that the later studies negated their supposed positive features, and their corrosive negative effects became apparent. The more investigators examined large schools, the worse conditions appeared. In 1990, thirty-one years after Conant had made his original proposal, a review of the research literature concluded:

> Today, small is related to school effectiveness, community and school identity, and individual fulfillment and participation. Big corresponds with school inefficiency, institutional bureaucracy and personal loneliness.[6]

Unfortunately, while Conant's proposals were in their ascendancy, the nation was saddled with thousands of massive schools. They remain today, particularly in the inner cities where education reaches its nadir.

Despite the unforeseen effects of Conant's ideas, his contentions were not completely wrong. Smaller schools can have adverse features. A summary of the Montgomery County study concluded that schools with a small number of pupils "had staffing problems because there were fewer staff members, students had little choice of teachers, there were fewer approaches to teaching, there was little use of specialists, and there were fewer books, materials, and pieces of equipment."[7]

Authorities today must choose between the gains and losses of large schools as opposed to smaller institutions. Computerized education will make the same positive features available in all schools while avoiding the negatives. Outstanding courses will be available everywhere. Since each student will be taught individually, it won't matter if one student is enrolled, or one hundred pupils take the same class.

Eventually, multiple smaller-learning enclaves will be able to eliminate the behemoths that alienate students today. Minimum size limits will be almost eliminated. In remote areas the school system could return to one-room establishments. The major difference between the old and new one-room schoolhouses is that the computer-based classrooms will be more conducive to expanded learning than any former school, large or small. Not only will students in every school have almost unlimited numbers of classes available, but they will also be hooked in electronically through the Internet with schools and resources worldwide. By telecommunications, children will discuss unlimited numbers of topics during their dozen pre-college years and be exposed to diverse viewpoints. They will evaluate ideas of other students, and their own work will be judged by their peers everywhere. They will exchange opinions with youth in areas and in countries that their parents, as students, could only read about in impersonal and inert textbooks. The relative size of the world is appreciably smaller, and diverse cultures understand each other better through immediate transmission of events on television news programs. These trends will be augmented as pupils correspond instantaneously with their peers in other lands and learn about them and from them. These interchanges will be supervised but will allow freedom to develop independent thinking and will be equally accessible in any school.

Other advantages will follow. The small schools can be located closer to the homes of the students to reduce travel time and busing costs. Many teaching materials will be more plentiful. The successors to today's CD-ROM disks will eventually provide expanded opportunities, and equipment will always be abundant and state-of-the-art as was illustrated in Chapter 14, which described computer simulation of microscopes and telescopes.

In recounting the pros and cons of large and small schools, I have said nothing about violence and vandalism that befoul many large institutions. The greater alienation of students is probably a contributor to the horrendous discipline problems of giant schools. The more extended a school becomes, the more impersonal it is, making education more difficult for students and authorities. Discipline can be better controlled when students feel more accountable for their actions as happens in smaller institutions. Peer pressure in a small school can be more beneficial and more easily enhanced.

Although studies show that students in small schools participate more in extracurricular activities, a possible problem could arise. Having fewer students in a school may conflict with the American penchant for winning varsity sports teams. Development of these better teams is aided by having more athletes available in a large school. Whether this demand for winning teams would be a difficulty is problematical. If, however, it does cause objections, smaller schools can be united in a group to form athletic teams. Where one large school now exists, five small schools can replace the monstrosity but with only one football team. The five small schools could be Adams1, Adams2, etc. The football team would go under the name of Adams. Even without athletics as the driving force for this arrangement, it may still be valuable. Bands and orchestras require more participants than can be found in a small school. Other activities might also benefit from occasional larger gatherings while keeping the basic small school structure.

Need for School Buildings

If children can learn from computers, why not let them stay home and plug into their machines? They could thereby be educated without the hassle of going to school and without the cost of schools to the community.

Chapter 3 includes reasons for retaining schools. In summary, schools enable students to develop social skills by interacting with other children, they furnish structure to ensure that students devote time to necessary studies, and they can develop and foster beneficial peer pressure to aid learning. Although, the home-schooling movement is able to overcome these obstacles, most parents would neither wish to take on the task, nor have the time and ability to do so.

Additional basic requirements for buildings flow from the role of teachers in computerized education. Although, theoretically, it might be possible for teachers to meet with students on an individual basis even if the children were not in schools, it would be extremely difficult. Moreover, for teachers to be able to conduct seminars and workshops, it is critical that students be able to gather in a central location, and this is usually the school building. For all these reasons, schools must remain.

School Configuration

Although buildings will remain, they will differ from present structures. The first and greatest change that computerized education will bring in schools will be to reduce their bloated dimensions; in addition, it will drastically and permanently transfigure the layout of classrooms. A computer will await the arrival of every pupil. Schools will need as many computers as attendees at one time. Machines will probably be set up next to each other, with their backs abutting the walls or the backs of other computers.

Classrooms can be larger than at present. The size of today's classroom is usually restricted by the need to teach only thirty students. That size has developed because teachers are at their wit's end when they try to impart knowledge to more than that number of pupils at one time. That difficulty will be eliminated when a computer tutors each student individually.

Where and when students take classes will be irrelevant. Only discipline and order will be important, but even these will differ from what present classrooms require. Rigid silence will be less necessary than today, although horseplay and unlimited interaction will always be interdicted. Under specified conditions, students will be permitted to change to another room or to another section or time period. Although students will each have a computer, they may use different ones at various times. By occasionally shifting machines and physical locations, pupils can meet other groups during school sessions. This will also allow certain computers with special capabilities to be used by different pupils and will avoid costs of duplicating the more expensive equipment needed for some lessons. The central computer in the school will handle all such scheduling.

Pupils will usually be assigned to a room for a given time although defined periods are not essential. Computers can download proper lesson material and can interact with a child wherever he or she happens to be. Each pupil will sign on to a machine at a specified time. The computer will have a record of subjects the student is to study. Instruction will begin exactly where the student ended in the previous session. The machine will make available the lessons that the pupil is to cover, and extra material on the subject will be accessible. Not all students will use additional subject matter but for those who have time and the interest to proceed further, supplemental opportunities will be available.

All computers will be connected on a network, and lessons and records will be kept on the central machine. That computer will maintain a record for each student. When each pupil logs in with the appropriate password, the machine will determine the subjects that are to be taken in each time period and will check the student's previous work to determine exactly where the lessons should begin. The material will be immediately available. A unique identification system like fingerprints or voiceprints could be used in the unlikely event that a protective device is needed.

The pupil will then begin the class and continue until the appointed stopping time. Class periods of equal length will probably continue in many schools because they allow students to be free at the same time and encourage informal interaction among them. Educators and researchers will decide the time that should be spent in each session by experience. Initially, length will probably be about the same as in present classes, but that may change in the future. Many options are possible.

The last class a student had may have been the previous day, or it may have been several days before if the student was sick. The lag between classes may have been even longer if the student took a vacation or was absent for other reasons. Pupils will have many justifications, such as workshops or seminars, for being away from school for periods of time. If the Leader Teacher has told the computer that the absence is legitimate, the computer will wait patiently for the student's return on the appointed day.

If a computer fails to work properly, the student could use the machine of an absent student in that room or another room. The correct study material can be downloaded to any computer.

Computers and programs are rapidly becoming ever more user friendly. Nonetheless, programming difficulties are inevitable. Most problems can be resolved through the instructions of the computer. When one arises that the student cannot readily solve by working with the available instructions and help from the software, someone who is familiar with the program will be needed. Similar difficulties happen in computer applications in business and experts, usually in the office of the software developer, are easily reached by phone. In schools, the same practice can be followed. When a problem, insoluble to the student arises, a computerized education expert will be available to the student by using the modem and phone. The expert will interact with the student to help unravel the difficulty. Technology is available for the computer specialist to appear on the screen and talk directly to a student. The outside expert can always develop a solution, whether permanent or temporary, even if that means simply telling the student to go to another lesson. A record of the problem will be recorded, and the information will be passed back to the programmers who devised the software. They can correct the glitch and download it to the school. Each upgrade will prevent similar future troubles.

It may happen that the computer expert will be tied up with another pupil when the call is made and will be unable to provide an immediate answer. The student's computer could hold that lesson in abeyance and proceed to another subject until the expert is able to return the call.

When each session is finished, a record of what was completed and other pertinent information will be uploaded back to the main computer. The machine will record the date, determine the material that should be relayed to the student for the next lesson, and note when that lesson should take place.

Students will receive all academic lessons by computer. Classes like physical education, where intellectual attainment is not essential, will continue unchanged with present methods.

A person will never be "teaching" in a classroom. A human will usually be present as a monitor or a facilitator to encourage learning and ensure that classroom behavior is appropriate. Discipline problems will always arise as youths grow into adulthood. Human monitors will deal with those obstacles to learning as is done today, and will notify the pupil's Leader Teacher when that is appropriate. These problems will be reduced sharply since computers are able to make learning much more enjoyable than in present classrooms. I have shown in Chapter 5 that increased student interest has resulted when computers have been used to instruct. This enhancement of the joy of learning will increase as computerized education progresses, for software can increasingly use psychological principles that will make learning even more stimulating and enjoyable.

Adjoining students may be taking the same course, but that will be irrelevant. All students could be studying different subjects in the same room. Even students taking the same course will usually be at different levels since students vary and have different learning rates.

At times, it will be advantageous for a group of students to work on a common project. The computers could schedule students to be in the same room simultaneously, provide the material, and prod students to solve the problem by group action.

When students are younger, human monitors will be more important. As students grow older, humans will still be necessary for many classes. The need for supervision, however, will diminish for some students, especially for those who become involved in intriguing projects. Computers have demonstrated repeatedly even under today's conditions, that they can totally absorb the attention of students. In certain classes with students that show few discipline problems, it will be possible to dispense with monitoring, partially or completely. Computers will keep accurate assessments of students and the work they are doing. If students require personal supervision to help them behave or learn well, the computer will quickly spot the errant pupils. They can easily be changed to a room with a human present.

Computers will check work accomplished by students in every class. If any problems develop, the Leader Teachers will be involved at once. Attendance will be mandatory, and figures will be available to authorities through computer records. Any unexplained truancy will be made known to the Leader Teacher, who will know the student well and will try to uncover causes and solutions.

As detailed above, multimedia will be an integral part of computerized education. Computers can use material either through a player on their own machine or through file servers. If the disk is used at the student's machine, record keeping will be similar to that of library books today. Computers could process paperwork needed to retrieve the disk, and it will be ready when the student comes to the library. The computer will keep a record of the loan until the disk is returned. Computers will "know" what material students will need for the next lesson and can tell them on the previous day to check out a specific disk from the library.

Computers will have modems. Safeguards against making unacceptable outside calls can be arranged. Access will require use of a password unique to each student and authorization of the central computer, which will ascertain if a student is in a course that necessitates a specific type of call. Numbers to which calls can be made could be specified.

Every computer will connect to at least one printer for necessary hard (printed) copies including homework assignments. For subjects like mathematics, copies of the problems will be taken home. For other subjects, the computer will print a list of the assigned reading material. In the next class, the computer will test immediately. This will serve as a check on whether homework had been done. The practice will also take advantage of the value of frequent testing as an aid to learning.

For those who have computers at home (and eventually they will be as common as TV sets are today), material from the computer at school can be downloaded to a disk and taken home. If they wish, pupils without computers will be able to remain after school and do "homework." This practice will be easier as schools become smaller, are located closer to students' homes, and busing is drastically curtailed or even eliminated.

Computers could be available to students in libraries for homework or to do additional work on subjects that interest them. Extra study by students can be expected since learning by its nature is enjoyable. Many instances have been recorded of students in classes today who use computers, and who want to continue their work on lessons when the class ends.[8]

Eventually, laptop or portable computers will be available for at least some students to take home with them. They might also be made available for pupils who will be absent for extended periods for various reasons with appropriate lesson material loaded in from the main school computer.

All students will be required, of course, to fulfill certain basic levels of achievement in fundamental courses. These will include reading, writing, math, science, foreign languages, and social studies.

Although students will neither receive grades nor go through a regular series of advancements such as moving from grade six to grade seven, the computer will show if he or she is making sufficient progress to complete the basic courses in the years allotted. A student who is moving at a satisfactory rate will be able to branch off when part of the course is particularly interesting. Students will be able to request additional learning materials in these subjects that intrigue them. For example, a student studying history might become interested in the various personages who appear. A simple request will cause the computer to search for available materials including multimedia presentations that will add immeasurably to the pleasure and enjoyment of following these inclinations.

A fear may arise that students will become hackers and raise havoc within the system. Banks, where computers manage billions of dollars have similar dangers, but they survive without untoward difficulty. Schools will also prosper despite this supposed threat. Exceptionally bright students who might be able to create some minor disruption will find their talents even more challenged as they progress at a much faster rate through the computer lessons. Moreover, with today's sophisticated computers and constantly updated programs, it will be a rare student who can effectively interfere with the system even to a small degree.

This chapter began with the studies of James Bryant Conant. Although some of his ideas about the value of large schools have been discounted, his eminent position in education remains. He was dedicated in his pursuit of better schools and better teaching. Conant was also a renowned scientist, recognized for his brilliant research. At the time of his death in 1978, personal computers were in their infancy. We can only speculate how this man of science with his passionate desire to improve education might have reacted if the opportunity had existed during his life to integrate modern science and technology with education. Advancements in computers now make it possible. One conclusion seems certain: Conant surely would have wanted to try something new if he were still here and had witnessed the futility of the changes in education since his original studies.

ADDITIONAL
CONSIDERATIONS

Chapter 22

Grades

*L*etter (or number) grades and schooling seem inseparable. A suggestion that they be abolished meets with reactions ranging from disbelief to fear about simplistic proponents of outlandish ideas. Standard questions immediately arise. Would students study if they weren't enticed by a good grade or threatened by a poor one? If they aren't necessary, why are they used everywhere?

Perhaps grades will be around forever, but I think another alternative exists. Before we canonize them as irreplaceable, some queries are appropriate:

1. What are the benefits of grades?

2. Can grades ever have negative features that are detrimental to learning?

3. Are other means of achieving those same advantages in existence today?

4. Is it possible that better results might be attained without grades?

Underlying the whole investigation is the point that I have stressed repeatedly in this book: serious flaws are crippling attempts to educate youth for a new technological world, and current practices aren't curing them. That doesn't mean, of course, that change should be imposed merely to start something new. It does suggest that many established procedures should be carefully examined. After study, if grades prove to be totally beneficial they should be retained. Otherwise it might be better to modify them, or to discard them if something better can be found.

Benefits of Grades

Grades have many valuable features. Seeing the possibility of receiving a good or better mark, students often work more diligently. Reception of good grades provides a reward, and rewards are psychologically necessary for anyone trying to succeed in any type of endeavor.

Grades also allow teachers, students, and parents to judge whether students are progressing properly. Teachers can judge which students need additional help during a course, and which are ready to be advanced at its conclusion. Grades help students judge whether they are succeeding. If they are failing, they obviously need more work. Even if they are getting by, prospects of receiving a lower grade than is desirable might push them to do more studying.

A report card with its curt but definitive set of marks is a believable signpost on which parents can rely. The suggestion to eliminate grades distresses guardians because of the value of knowing how their children are performing in school. Grades enable them to reward good efforts, or to encourage their children to study more when necessary.

These advantages are reasons that grades have endured in education for centuries, despite occasional attempts to dispense with them. The more important reason grades remain is because until now, no other suitable way of achieving similar results has been found. This is an important answer to the rhetorical question asked a few paragraphs back about why they are used universally if they are unnecessary. Lack of an alternative has also been the justification for overlooking the inherent problems connected with grades. Now that technology makes it possible to dispense with them, their true value, including their disadvantages, needs to be studied.

Disadvantages of Grades

One negative complication of grades is that they depend not only on students but also on teachers. Similar marks may signify varied accomplishments if given by different instructors. Some teachers achieve a reputation for giving good grades without requiring much work. An unfortunate consequence is that students sometimes choose teachers because of the probable grade instead of what they will learn.

Even the same instructor assigning grades will not always evaluate the work of every student with equal impartiality. The possibility of bias and prejudice, whether positive or negative, is always a danger whenever a grade depends in any way upon a subjective judgment of a teacher, and that happens frequently. As was said earlier, bias may not be deliberate and may exist even if the instructor is not conscious of it.

Grades are dependent not only on teachers but also on the standards of schools, and these differ widely. Students at times transfer to another school and find that they have learned less than their new classmates although they received satisfactory marks in their prior school. A grade in one location may have a different connotation than the same one in another school. Neither may accurately reflect how much learning has taken place. Grades may allow a student, parents, and teachers to see how well the student is doing as contrasted with the rest of the class without showing the quality of the education. This failure to evaluate schooling is particularly important today. Although many people are aware that American schools in general are producing inferior results, most parents feel that *their* child is receiving a good education. The grades their children receive contribute to this mistaken security. When they receive a report card with high marks, they never realize their children could be receiving a poor education when judged by international standards.

Grades show nothing about the knowledge that students would have acquired in a different school or with another teacher or under diverse circumstances. The drop in SAT scores at prestigious schools is a serious problem. Students entering those schools have probably been getting as many A's as their predecessors; despite equal grades, their learning is less than that of former students.

A major difficulty with grades is the confusion they engender between true learning and the reception of a grade. Hope of a good mark instead of a desire for learning generates many inappropriate behaviors in schools. The common practice of "cramming" for tests illustrates the evil of stressing grades as opposed to learning. Research on the Spacing Effect mentioned in Chapter 13 shows that cramming is an ineffective learning tool. Although it may not be much help to learning, students use the practice widely and justifiably swear by its value for getting better marks, and students are judged on grades, not on learning.

Grades have the further disadvantage that they may give a distorted picture of what is success. Many students who have received poor marks in school have done well, while others who have received good ones have discovered that life in the world is different from life in a school. Some students develop a knack for achieving good grades and not always because they learn exceptionally well.

Grades measure one type of intelligence, but intelligence is now known to be a multifaceted trait. The demand for good marks often outweighs the esteem of other talents.

None of these shortcomings are as damaging as another serious drawback: they can devastate self-esteem. While an A or B may be rewarding, a D or F is not. These lower marks are punishing. Punishment can sometimes be used effectively, but vast amounts of research show that the outcome of punishment is difficult to control or predetermine. While an F might increase effort, it will more likely have the opposite effect and demoralize the student. A succession of low grades will lead inevitably to complete discouragement.

Although the immediate conclusion of an onlooker seeing a low grade might be that the student needed to try harder, that assumption could be false. Many causes, including failure of schools to teach children to read well, could result in low marks. Lack of effort by students may bring poor grades, but it is only one of many possible causes.

The negative effect of poor grades was voiced by educational researchers at a conference on student motivation sponsored by the Office of Educational Research and Improvement (OERI). They concluded:

> Because high ability students usually capture the best grades and test scores, the labor of less-talented students is seldom acknowledged and the grades they receive for it do not inspire effort. Hence, low-ability students and those who are disadvantaged—students who must work harder—have the least incentive to do so. They find this relationship between high effort and low grades unacceptable, something to be evaded if possible. Some of them express their displeasure by simple indifference, others by disruption and deception.[1]

No one has proposed a viable solution for this dilemma, and none is foreseeable as long as grades retain their present position in education.

Obviously, grades are not perfect, nor are they indispensable. Computerized education can eliminate them, but to justify abolishing them or even modifying them radically, their authentic advantages must be accounted for in another way.

Learning Without Grades

The value of grades can be summarized under two major headings:

1. They stimulate students to work harder either by providing rewards or by threatening to punish anyone who performs poorly.
2. Grades allow students, teachers, and parents to form an evaluation of the progress students are making, even if their conclusions are sometimes mistaken.

Rehashing the capability of computers to provide rewards would be superfluous. Computerized education fills this human need better than grades can ever accomplish, as noted in Chapter 12. It applies to better students, to slower students, to all students.

Computerized education will eliminate the punishment of low grades. It may seem contradictory but with computers, rewards will replace most penalties. Even if a student falls behind the standards of what should be accomplished, computers will seek something to praise rather than to criticize. Critics may dismiss this outlook as too idealistic. They forget that rewards are much greater stimuli to improvement than punishment. The more students achieve, the more likely they will be to strive further. The present method of punishing poor students is unsuccessful. Twenty-five million illiterates in the nation received a liberal dose of poor grades. They remain illiterate. Students in the Florida at-risk programs had been receiving punishments in the form of low grades for many years. Their poor performance continued. When they began to be rewarded for their successes, their accomplishments increased beyond expectations.

Any educational system should judge the progress of students by their learning. Since grades do not always express this, they cannot be accurate indicators. Reports from computer schools will overcome this weakness because results will show that the student has mastered a specified amount of material. It won't say that the child received an A or a C but will reflect how completion of this subject matter accords with what is necessary for the child to be graduated by a suitable age and the course's relation to other goals established for the student.

Different students will embrace individual objectives. Some may be planning to stop their education at age eighteen. Others may plan to go on to higher education. Requirements and norms will depend on goals, but students will be able to strive for any objective and also to change as they progress. Underlying the variations will be certain standards that all students will be expected to complete in the basic subjects of English and other languages, math, sciences, history, and geography. Computers will be able to make this information about progress continually available to Leader Teachers. They, in turn, will be able to relay it to parents in their meetings, or through mail as report cards are sent today. The teachers will also, of course, reinforce students by praising their gains.

Parents will know how their child's growth in learning corresponds with what should be expected as a minimum, but also what students similar to their child will attain. The computer reports will present a more extensive review of what the child is accomplishing, where his or her particular strengths lie, and what kind of additional studies might be profitable.

If the student is showing extra ability, the computer will do more than simply award an A. It will direct and encourage the child to build on this capability. An example is mathematics. Those students who master sufficient arithmetic to begin algebra could do so whatever their age might be, and regardless of the time it took to reach that mastery. It will also be irrelevant at what time in the semester the achievement takes place. When algebra is completed, further advanced math courses will be available. Standard courses will be given in a regular order, but age will not bind students into preset patterns.

Students will not only be aware of their progress toward minimum learning requirements that will enable them to graduate, but they will also know how they compare with ordinary and exceptional students in many subjects, including those that might interest them as a possible life work. If a subject excites a student, it will be valuable to know how he or she matches up with other students who also might be thinking of a future in the field. Occasionally a comparison might point out that a student is poorly qualified. More likely, it will create another inducement to continue or, at least, point out improvements that will be needed. Usually, students become intrigued by subjects in which they have talents, and additional encouragement can only be beneficial.

While students will always be rewarded, they must look at their accomplishments realistically and honestly. They will be able to see how they compare with students not only throughout the country but also in other nations. It will be helpful if pupils, especially the brighter ones, understand that they have intense competition in every nation. They need to be reminded that the world is larger than the physical boundaries of the school they happen to attend.

Computerized education will be geared to prevent students from falling behind. If a student does fail to achieve enough for his or her age level, the Leader Teacher will be made aware of it through the regular computer progress report. The teacher may then wish to involve outside resources if other problems such as drugs or illness exist. Parents will likewise be informed.

Computerized education will help to equalize opportunities because computers can teach the same everywhere with equivalent software. National norms for necessary education will be easier to establish. Although grades will be eliminated, national tests will still be valuable. The SAT exam is helpful for college admissions and will pose no difficulty.

In summary, computerized education can eliminate grades and still provide the two predominant contributions that grades make to education: rewards and notification of progress. Computerized education will accomplish both assignments better than grades. Computers will also eliminate the shortcomings of grades: their indications of progress will not be dependent on variations of individual teachers; they will show progress in actual learning, and can be based on the same criteria for all students; by eliminating most punishments, they will focus on building positive reinforcement.

Dropping Class Grades

This chapter has concentrated on letter grades, but class grades, like fifth grade or ninth grade, will likewise be eliminated. These are artificial molds in which schools must confine children because they have no other option without individual tutors. Good education could dispense with them without harm. Alexander the Great didn't feel slighted because Aristotle didn't move him along at the same pace as the other students in Macedonia.

In computerized education, each academic subject will have a series of accomplishments needed to complete the course. Students have different abilities and their rate of advancement should and will vary. Pupils today cannot progress at dissimilar speeds because each class must move in lock step unison to cover each course of the curriculum in the allotted time. The individualized instruction of computerized education will allow students to advance at precisely the rate that will be advantageous for them. Predetermined schedules will not govern their progress, nor will their advancement depend on the abilities of other pupils. Some will move faster, some slower. Some will show more skill in one type of course, but the same students may be weaker in other subjects.

Since grouping children according to similar chronological levels is advantageous, age will be the criterion for placement of children in schools. The number of age levels in each school can be adjusted according to the needs of the locality. The value of neighborhood schools will be an important consideration. Individual systems may want more or fewer age groups in one location than will be helpful elsewhere. Age divisions will depend on local conditions but will be irrelevant to the schooling that children receive.

Grouping children only by age and teaching them individually will prevent the destructive practice frequently found today: schools pass children despite their lack of preparation for what will be taught in the next grade. As was mentioned above, the result of this system is that students can be graduated but still not be educated. Schools, however, often have few alternatives, and they confront an impossible dilemma. If they advance the child without sufficient learning, he or she is unprepared for what will be taught in the next class. If they do not move the student to the next grade, the child is an obvious failure with consequent damage to his or her self-esteem and will be out of place with younger children.

This difficulty hinders not only students who are totally behind in their studies but also affects those who are only deficient in one or a few areas. Even when a child is able to do some work for the next grade, he or she may be unable to do all necessary work. A student, for example, may have mastered the writing skills and the history lessons for grade four but may not have succeeded in the struggle with mathematics for that grade. Sometimes an attempt is made in summer school to help bridge that gap. Often the choice comes down to keeping students in grade four, where they have already mastered part of the material, or sending them to grade five, where they will be at a disadvantage in one or more subjects. This problem will cease with computerized education. Children will be where they should be chronologically, and the computer software will be teaching them exactly what they need to learn next in the progression toward graduation.

In the initial years of computerized education, abolishing artificial grade differentiations will be particularly important because extensive remedial instruction will be necessary. Students who are older will still be studying subjects that will be taken only by much younger students after computerized education has made its impact felt in schools. After the present formidable weaknesses of students are worked out, variations in course work will be less pronounced. Whether the differences are large or small, however, computerized education can manage them without class grades.

After computerized education is established, virtually all students will be able to meet the basic standards. Then divergences will develop because certain students will be able to progress much faster and will be doing more advanced work in fields that interest them. That variation will not hinder students. Children of the same age could be in the same school and in the same classrooms but be working on much different studies.

Conclusion

This chapter began with the question of possible elimination of a venerable tradition in schools: letter grades. It has been expanded to include class grades. After examination, proposals to eliminate both forms of grades prove to be reasonable. When grades exit from schools, their benefits and strong points will remain, but their inherent problems will disappear.

Chapter 23

Better Thinking

*A*nother complaint is leveled at education: students are not taught to think well. Authors assign various names to the desired activity including "critical thinking," "higher-order thinking," or "improved reasoning." Although writers use these terms differently, a basic idea is that students need to be able to progress from knowledge of facts to arrive at more complex conclusions through intellectual activity. For simplicity, I'll use the terms interchangeably and synonymously because of their common foundation.

One explanation why development of higher-order thinking is weak is that many children are poorly educated. Everyone must have basic information before trying to advance to further conclusions. If students lack sound learning foundations, they can't use facts as the stepping stones to advanced reasoning. With hundreds of thousands of illiterate students leaving the school system each year, many obviously aren't acquiring sufficient basic knowledge upon which they can build a better system of thinking. Improving basic education is, therefore, a major priority in attempts to develop advanced thinking.

Where suitable education is in place, educational writers stress the need for teachers to formulate and use penetrating oral questions to develop reasoned thinking.[1] Although this theory is excellent, carrying it out creates a familiar problem for teachers. Widely different levels of student ability and knowledge appear in every class. No individual question can be equally helpful to all pupils simultaneously. Questions that aid some students may be too elementary or excessively difficult for others.

The diversity among student abilities has its usual counterpart among teachers who have different abilities and skills. Developing good questions is an art. Certain instructors have greater talent for creating thought-provoking questions; some also have more ability in posing their questions to the class.

Educators caution about a potential hazard in recitations. Many teachers find it difficult to allow sufficient time for students to think seriously about what they will say in response to questions. This time to answer questions is "wait time" or the interval the teacher gives students to answer before another question or an evaluation of a response is given. Some teachers have a tendency to abbreviate this period. Quick reactions prevent uncomfortable pauses that might bore the students who are not responding. The unfortunate result is that shorter wait time makes it more difficult for students to become accustomed to think thoroughly about questions.

Readers who have progressed this far in this book suspect they know what is coming next. They probably think I am going to try to show that computerized education can develop higher-order thinking and can do it better than today's system. Those of you who have come to this conclusion have exercised your thinking skills well and you are correct. I think computerized education will be far more efficacious for developing better reasoning in students.

Keep in mind three of the requirements mentioned for developing improved thinking: a good underlying education, thought-provoking questions, and sufficient time for students to think before responding. Computers can manage these assignments with ease.

I have discussed in many places in this book why computerized education can provide superior learning for students.

Beyond the need for better education, good questioning is also important with computers as with individual teachers. Students must have an impetus to take information they have acquired and use it as the basis of developing their reasoning powers. Thought-provoking questions aid this process. Computers can be programmed to ask stimulating questions with varying levels of difficulty that can be effective with different types of students.

This possibility of computers querying pupils may bring hesitation among readers who will have a couple of immediate questions themselves. Can computers correct the answers to the questions that are beyond mere multiple choice queries? If computers must use multiple choice questions, can these help to develop thinking?

I'll start with the second part about the value of multiple choice questions that computers can obviously provide. A major difficulty with many questions found on today's tests is their poor quality. Many quizzes are not ideally constructed.[2] Consequently, the value of these questions cannot go beyond their inherent weaknesses. When programmers can have a few knowledgeable and astute people formulate questions, these queries will be of consistently high quality. Moreover, all computer questions possess an advantage of enormous value: each answer can be immediately corrected and feedback given. This capability of a rapid response and follow up to every answer of every student is a magnificent learning tool. When combined with well-formulated questions it can aid development of critical thinking to a degree that is difficult to duplicate except through individual tutors.

Satisfactory responses will bring additional questions aimed at helping students use their reasoning powers. If an incorrect answer is chosen, the computer can provide an explanation of the error. An additional question or questions can be immediately presented. Multiple choice questions, used this way, can lead students to understand material well, and are able to teach them to think better.

Now we can return to the first question about the ability of computers to correct and evaluate responses to other types of questions. Software gives computers unequalled versatility that will allow them in the future to go beyond multiple choice questions. The gargantuan memories of the machines combined with their immense power and speed will make it possible to analyze many types of responses. Programmers working with educators will develop many of the correct or applicable answers to questions, and store them in the machine's memory. Computers will read a student's answer and compare it with what is in its memory. Students will not have to write exactly what is stored, but the computer will scan their answers for key words and phrases. By that, the machines can help guide pupils toward the crucial responses that accompany higher order thinking.

Although computers can analyze some answers today, this machine skill is in its infancy and will improve as computerized education is more widely used. Programmers will receive continual feedback about the results of software. I have commented upon effects of this return of data in Chapters 6, 7, and 13.

Programmers will be informed about answers that students made to queries with the subsequent response that the computer provided. These replies can then be studied by educators and programmers to decide how the computer could improve its methodology and how it could augment better thinking by students. Upgrades to software will be ongoing, and the teaching skills of computers will continually advance.

A further comment about correction of answers is fitting here. Questions are intended to stimulate students to think. Analysis of answers will ensure that incorrect or frivolous responses are noticed, but they have a more important use: to direct students to delve deeper into problems. As in other phases of computerized education, answers will be ungraded. Questions, in this context, are meant to help students to think better and thus to improve reasoning, not to develop a grade.

A potential objection to use of computers follows from benefits that class discussions provide pupils. A difficulty for computers seems to be their emphasis upon individual instruction that eliminates exchanges between students. Class discussion, however, will predominate in seminars and workshops, which were discussed especially in Chapter 19. These will form a crucial element in computerized education. Moreover, students will be taking seminars in subjects that appeal to them. This will enable them to become better involved in the dialogues. Teachers who lead seminars and workshops will also have more time to develop these projects.

In addition, instruction that is done individually can provide some of the positive features of discussions by other means. Programmers can film sessions with students responding to questions but edit the films, allowing the pace to move rapidly to foster student interest. At any point, the computer could stop the film and request the student to respond to a question. Either the computer could comment on the reply immediately or could introduce the answers of other students in the film.

Moreover, computers have two advantages over ordinary classroom recitations. Students will be able to respond to all questions, and answers will be given privately. Not every one of thirty students in today's classroom can participate vocally in every recitation. Time is always scarce; as one student takes time to respond, every other pupil has less time available. All students in computerized education will be able to reply to every question.

Both shy and slow students are hesitant to voice their opinions voluntarily in class recitations for fear their peers will ridicule them and their answers. Computers are private. When students are formulating their responses, they don't need to be afraid of how they will appear before others. For some students, this will be crucial in helping them develop their thinking skills.

Computers can also be programmed to provide sufficient time to allow students to think out their answers. Wait time can vary and be adapted to the ability of the student. Sufficient time will always be available to aid pupils to profit from thought provoking questions.

Mathematics

What has been said thus far in this chapter explains how computers can develop higher-order thinking in social studies types of classes. Mathematical reasoning has a somewhat different form. One crucial key to mastering advanced thinking in mathematics is found in the student's ability to solve word problems. These provide an important step beyond simple calculations. Initially, students must learn to arrive at solutions to basic problems such as:

$$89 \times .85 = ?$$

The more important question is whether the child can understand how to solve a word problem with the same figures:

> Mary wants to buy a chair that costs eighty-nine dollars, but the most she can afford is eighty dollars. A few days later the store advertises a sale and says that everyone buying furniture will receive a 15 percent discount. Can she now afford the chair? How much will it now cost her?

This problem, of course, is elementary, but the same basic difficulties are present in all word problems whatever their complexity. Children must make the jump from knowledge of unadorned mathematics to the more important understanding of how to solve problems that contain words. These bring students into the world of higher-order thinking, an essential step to master mathematics.

Some students, especially the better ones, have no difficulty in immediately adapting to word problems. Bright students usually find them interesting and absorbing. Their natural curiosity impels them to try to find solutions. Other students, however, find word problems to be a daunting barrier. They need individual instruction and must begin at the simplest level. They can be taught, however, to make advances in solving word problems. It takes patience and time. Teachers have patience, but they seldom have enough time to help all students fully. Computers have both time and patience.

Teaching higher-order thinking to pupils with the greatest difficulty in mathematical problems requires individual instruction. The computer can quickly analyze every incorrect answer. Some errors may suggest merely a calculation slip. The correct answer to the problem about Mary's chair is $75.65. The computer would recognize an answer of "$74.65" as merely a computational error, and the student would be asked to check on the figures.

Other errors will show a more fundamental problem. Sometimes one incorrect answer may be insufficient to diagnose the type of error. The computer can provide more questions and address possibilities until it finds the key to the mistake. It can then concentrate on providing a remedy for the difficulty. A computer has unique advantages in teaching students to solve these problems because of its ability to be an individual tutor combined with its infinite patience and capacity to keep students interested through rewards.

Computers will be able to break problems into small segments and to formulate questions. They will take students through each level and with as many problems as necessary until pupils begin to understand better. A human teacher could do the same if he or she had only one child in class.

Geometry is a form of mathematics that requires extensive use of higher-order thinking. The Congressional Office of Technology has commented on one computer program that has been developed to teach the subject. It illustrates some possibilities of computerized education.

> The Geometry Tutor is an intelligent tutoring system that employs audit trails and is currently under study at Carnegie-Mellon University's Advanced Computer Tutoring Project. It provides instruction in proving geometry theorems and focuses on teaching

students to problem solve and to plan when they prove theorems. According to the authors of the Geometry Tutor, these skills are seldom emphasized in a standard geometry curriculum. Students often complete a geometry course with only a modest ability to generate proofs and little deep understanding of the nature of proofs. The Geometry Tutor monitors students while they are actually engaged in solving the problems and provides instruction and guidance during the problem solving process. Students do not have to wait until their papers are corrected to receive feedback. Feedback is immediate, precise, instructionally relevant, and based on a more thorough analysis of problem solving behavior than would be possible with one teacher and a classroom full of students. The Geometry Tutor was initially tested on a few high school students, some who had no geometry instruction and some who had just completed a high school geometry course. After 10 hours of instruction, all students were able to solve problems that their teachers considered too difficult to assign to their classes. In fact, a student who had almost failed geometry was successful and the students considered their time on the computer as fun.[3]

This provides a graphic example of the basic contention of this chapter: computers can develop higher-order thinking.

This chapter began with a comment that critics complain about a lack of instruction in schools that can develop better thinking. Educators should not decry the inadequacy of teaching thinking skills under the difficult conditions that teachers face today. Rather, they should express sad astonishment that the preeminent teaching tool of all ages is being neglected. Computerized education could help schools make giant strides in their efforts to produce students who can use advanced thinking.

Chapter 24

Paying for Computerized Education

Computers, properly used, can vastly improve education everywhere. Even if the price of this advanced educational system were substantially higher, it would be worth it. Consequently, the primary reason schools should adopt computerized education is not to save money but to improve learning. Nonetheless, full use of computers will eventually bring substantial monetary savings.

For those who are seeking reasons why computerized education is impossible, a seemingly unanswerable objection is the cost of millions of new computers, software, and new wiring for school buildings. A computer must be provided for every student and school budgets are already stretched to the limit. Opponents will object that these costs are prohibitive.

What will computerized education cost? An important contributor to the widespread use of computers has been the spectacular increase in power and speed that has been coupled with lower and lower cost. If automobiles had progressed the way computers have, it would probably be possible to buy a car that sped along at over five hundred miles an hour for five hundred dollars and get five hundred miles per gallon. While the quality of computers has soared, their price has been plummeting year after year, up to 35 percent in one year. With these continuing reductions, less than one thousand dollars would provide a quality machine and monitor, while allowing for unexpected contingencies. Although each student will need an individual computer for their instruction, it is not necessary to have the total number of computers equal the total number of students. Class hours can be staggered and timing of seminars could be taken into account (by other computer programs) to reduce the number of machines in a school. Although upgrades to equipment are made continuously, it is not necessary to replace all hardware every time an advance is made. Computers and software should last for an average of four years, and improved wiring is a one-time cost.

The cost of software is hard to determine, but it is certain that competition will quickly lessen this expenditure as more schools embrace computerized education. To this must be added costs of networking, special computer paraphernalia, and multimedia equipment. The total cost will probably not exceed two thousand dollars per student. Based on these figures, the cost to the schools would be approximately five hundred dollars per year per student over the four-year period, a tiny sum to spend for the benefits that will accrue. The lack of total significance of this figure becomes more apparent when contrasted with what inferior education is costing today.

Remedial education in industry is a multi billion-dollar undertaking today. The article, cited above in the *New York Times*[71], placed the cost at about thirty billion dollars per year. Although that figure is probably exaggerated, the yearly cost to business certainly goes into the billions, and every billion translates into twenty-five dollars for each of the forty million students in schools. Those total savings will be delayed because the present educational system has burdened the nation with twenty-five million illiterates who still must be helped. Nonetheless, substantial dollar savings will result and will increase yearly; these savings will make costs of computerized education seem even less important.

Business obviously is willing to contribute to improved education as its multibillion-dollar expenditure shows. The difficulty until now has been that major improvements have been non-existent, and this condition discourages industry from increasing their assistance to schools. When schools are graduating students who are prepared educationally, business will be able to achieve meaningful savings because expenditures they make to provide remedial education will diminish sharply. Business wants these savings, and if they could see promise that schools will improve, they would probably be willing to pay for it through additional taxes.

Although there will be initial costs, there will also be immediate savings, which will continue to increase. Eventually these will reduce expenditures below present cost.

Potential Savings

1. **Reduction in the cost of substitute teachers**. In Chapter 16 the
   elimination of substitute teachers in computer schools was detailed.
   This will bring an immediate dollar savings. Substitute teachers cost
   schools about 2 percent of their annual budget. If the average
   student cost is five thousand dollars per year, one hundred dollars
   per year will be saved from eliminating substitute teachers, or, by
   itself, about one fifth of the total yearly cost of computerized education.

2. **Reduction of Non-teaching Personnel**. Smaller schools combined
   with students who are finding education more enjoyable will reduce
   discipline problems, which are costly for schools today. Improved
   behavior will make life easier and better for teachers and will also
   lessen the number of non-teaching employees that will be needed.
   Disciplinary and security personnel will be decreased. Truancy and
   the need for workers to track down truants will also be diminished.
   Non-teaching personnel must provide substitute teachers throughout the system. This includes those who must find and sign up subs
   and those who must complete the daily chore of making sure that
   every class is covered. When substitute teaching is eliminated,
   lessening of this staff will be possible. Computers will cut paperwork
   not only for teachers but also for schools. This will reduce the
   number of non-teaching personnel needed.

3. **Less Vandalism**. Schools are damaged. Repairs cost money. Better
   discipline will save substantial amounts of money.

4. **Better Use of School Buildings**. Savings will be realized eventually
   because buildings will be used more efficiently, and fewer classrooms
   will be needed. At present, schools are used at close to 100 percent
   capacity from 8:30 AM until 3:00 PM for about nine months of the year
   and at a sharply lower rate during the other months. Computer
   schools could be open from 6:00 AM until 9:00 PM for twelve months of
   every year. Older students would be more likely to opt for later or
   earlier hours if they wanted to work part time. Schools usually avoid

staggered hours today because of scheduling, supervision, and teaching constraints. Computers will make these difficulties less important. Students wishing to take advantage of later hours will be prepared to require less monitoring, as could be expected from those students who have matured. Effective self-directed learning is always desirable in education, and this will be another opportunity for advanced students to achieve this goal. Any student who is unable to work without a monitor will forego classes taken at unusual hours. Classrooms could be monitored by video cameras, but that would be for safety reasons.

5. **Less Busing**. Schools will be much smaller and will be located much closer to homes of students as noted in Chapter 21. Busing has become a major expense in recent years, and proximity of homes to schools will dramatically lessen these costs.

6. **Reduced Textbook Costs**. Although some printed textbooks will probably continue, they will often be smaller, be used less, and be of diminished importance than at present. Many will be replaced. One small CD-ROM disk can provide as much text as several books. In 1991, World Library published over 950 works of authors from Plato to Poe on one disk. In 1994, they brought out a revised version, still on only one disk, that contained 1750 titles plus multi media additions and included the complete Bible. Now complete encyclopedias are found on one or two disks. As the inexorable advances in computer technology take place, CD-ROMs are nearing obsolescence. They will be replaced, probably initially by Digital Video Disks (DVD), which will bring at least another twentyfold increase in storage capacity. Although remuneration of authors and profit for publishers should be about the same for books or disks, a large part of the expense of books is for paper and printing. With CD-ROM or DVD technology, the basic cost of the material is insignificant compared to the cost of textbooks. Savings will also accrue from the reduced expenses of storage, transportation and disposal. Moreover, use of paper, ink, and printing of textbooks limits their flexibility and ultimately raises their costs. A substantial number of textbooks

must be printed to offset initial setup costs. When an error is discovered in the text as has happened occasionally in recent years, the error can only be erased by destroying the book. DVD's will be alterable, just as other software can be readily changed without discarding the disks. As new information becomes available, it can be added quickly. Changes can be made through telephone lines and modems. One recommendation of a commission studying education that Ross Perot headed in Texas was to reduce the time for texts used from eight years to from four to six years.[72] That will never be an issue with software since it will be updated continually.

7. **Better Teacher Morale**. An important source of saving in computerized education is difficult to quantify: improved morale among teachers. Under present conditions, teachers must contend with many pupils who are ill prepared to do the necessary work because they have gotten behind in an earlier class. That poses an insurmountable and devastating obstacle for someone sincerely trying to help children to learn. Teachers must likewise contend with discipline problems that are magnified because students are unable to advance in school and seek other outlets for their need to succeed. Poor morale and consequent burnout contributes to turnover among teachers. Turnover is a major expense among businesses and is costly for schools also although it is often overlooked. Poor morale eventually leads to higher medical costs for many teachers. Consequently, better morale will bring important monetary savings to school systems.

8. **Reduction of Crime Expense**. The cost of crime and prisons is astronomical. The connection between illiteracy and crime was noted above in Chapter 1. The "social dynamite" that James Bryant Conant saw as the result of inferior education has resulted in riots only in the inner cities. Middle class citizens, secure in their enclaves, rue the damage and bloodshed, but the violence hasn't yet hurt them or their families or their homes. Eventually, they too will suffer from mob ferocity unless something is done about an education system that frequently embitters its victims. Every nation can and must eliminate growing class distinctions based on education.

Computers can educate everybody. Failure to do this will cost more in dollars than can be imagined.

The cost of converting education to computerized education is not large under any system of accounting that considers what the present system is costing. In addition, however, actual dollar savings will reduce these initial costs appreciably and will eventually generate true gains over present practices. In summation, the goal of establishing computerized education is not primarily to save money. Nonetheless, that will be an important result.

Chapter 25

Replication

*T*he ultimate value of any innovation depends on whether it can generate similar results when used in another location. Scientists refer to this transference as replication. This characteristic is especially important in education where new methods are desperately needed.

Highly creative teachers struggle continually to improve the educational system. This leads to new and original methods of teaching in individual classes with excellent results. When a promising new teaching method is developed, it often comes to the attention of the authorities. They want the better method to be copied to bring the gains to other classes, and they often try to make it known to other teachers. When an attempt is made to have other teachers emulate the new approach in other classes or different schools, the results often fall short of expectations and hopes.

The teacher who devised the new program can use his or her unique method with different students and in other schools. If other teachers who try to use the method achieve inferior results, something is different in the classrooms of the teacher who is successful and those who are unable to reach the same success. These crucial divergences must reside within the teachers.

The problem that has reappeared often in this book—the varied talents found in millions of teachers—is again the culprit. The basic hindrance to replication in education is that teachers are different, and education is dependent upon their individual skills. These variations among instructors prevent many valuable techniques from being repeated.

Some differences among teachers are obvious. For example, one teacher may have more skills in keeping a class interested in the material being taught.

Another may be more adept in encouraging students to feel they can learn. A third may be better able to diagnose weaknesses in students from answers given. These are only a few of innumerable diverse traits that a skilled observer might deduce from watching teachers. Also present are other subtle variations that observers can't recognize and other teachers can't copy. The number of possible critical differences between one teacher and another is virtually unlimited.

When researchers in sciences perform experiments, they must control for elements that may affect outcomes but may differ according to the subjects. For example, to judge which of two academic classes is more successful, the testers must ensure that the intelligence levels of the subjects in the two classes are approximately the same, or else they must account for those differences (called variables) when evaluating the outcome. Failure to do this results in poor research with flawed or meaningless conclusions.

Researchers need to control as many variables as possible when arranging any type of experiment. In evaluating and repeating teaching methods, the differences among teachers need to be accounted for. Since many are unknown or unrecognized, they cannot be controlled making it impossible for researchers to pinpoint exactly what teacher characteristics are necessary to make a new program succeed. The result is that an idea that one teacher uses successfully fails to help others, and researchers are unable to determine exactly why this is.

Hindrances to replicating individual classes are multiplied when attempts are made to duplicate new forms of schools. Difficulties are increased because many teachers and officials are part of the new undertaking. Consequently, the number of variables is expanded.

Besides the individual differences, another important element is usually present when radically new ventures are attempted. Many people, especially innovators, benefit from an intense drive that motivates them when they are embarking upon something new and exciting. That same drive and excitement is absent in others who merely try to imitate what has already been accomplished. New and groundbreaking schools usually begin with one or a few zealous and creative teachers or administrators who are driven by a new idea. These innovators then convince other teachers and authorities of the value of the system and that the new program can assist education. After this intense preparation is completed, the new approach is tried. Often it succeeds.

Publication of *A Nation At Risk* in 1983 intensified the search for new methods, and many original teaching practices have been started in the last fifteen years. Often these new schools have been successful. They have achieved noteworthy results and frequently receive nationwide publicity. The TV networks often do stories on them. National magazines do the same. Enough new programs are available to keep the media occupied because of the many creative attempts.

These novel learning environments are seldom repeated. If they are tried elsewhere, results often fall short of those in the beginning program. Few new experiments go much beyond the school or district where they begin. The reason is simple: other teachers and authorities in other schools lack the individual characteristics and founding zeal of people driving the original accomplishments. Consequently, the schools cannot be repeated with equal success.

I mentioned above that the introduction of blackboards seems to be the main innovation that has had universal acceptance in education in the last hundred years. They were a good idea, of course, but reformers have proposed many good ideas during that same time. Blackboards were accepted because they are independent of the individual traits of teachers. They are purely physical and can be used by all teachers; they are unaffected by individual talents and skills.

While the extreme difficulty of replicating new and innovative programs is a severe hindrance in making drastic changes in today's educational picture, easy replication is a prominent advantage of computerized education. This system is not dependent upon the varied skills and talents of teachers and administrators but upon software.

Innovation can be duplicated since software can be the same in all computers. Educators, working with programmers, can and will develop new programs. The combination of the resources of the two groups will create radically new and exciting breakthroughs in learning. When a new program proves successful in one classroom, it will bring equal benefits in another, just as the same teacher can succeed with his or her teaching method in different classes and schools. A computer program that is able to teach well will never lose its value. It will not retire or die but will only be improved.

The capability of being replicated is apparent in the Florida at-risk programs. Vero Beach began its innovative approach in 1987. Within four years the program had appeared in twenty locations within Florida and in other schools outside Florida. Replication is rare in education, and new ideas ordinarily don't spread that rapidly. Not only was the computer system duplicated throughout the state but the results in other schools were also equally impressive, another rare phenomenon in education.

The ability of computer teaching to be duplicated exactly in other locations differs from rigidity. Computerized education will have unequalled versatility. A technique that can successfully teach many pupils in different schools may still not be perfect for every student. Needs of students will determine which programs are used. When a pupil does not learn, the computer will know it and will often be able to select another method.

The replicability of computerized education will add a new asset to schooling that will become ever more valuable as improvements in computers and software continue their inexorable advances.

Chapter 26

Inner-City Schools

*S*ociety stresses punishment as the remedy for crime. That cure is usually ineffective, but when terrorized citizens demand more cells, the government complies. It spends staggering sums to build prisons, yet lawlessness continues. If punishment could change evils, America with its unchallenged record of the most jail cells per citizen would also be the most law abiding nation on earth. The futility of trying to change society merely by increasing incarceration is particularly evident in the inner cities. A huge percentage of these residents spend time locked up, but crime in the inner cities is worse than in other areas.

People everywhere envy the freedom of Americans. Illegal immigrants use their lives as a stake in a gamble to achieve it, believing that if they succeed, they will then have a hope for happiness. For many Americans who live in the inner cities, there is no hope, new or old. Their supposed benefits of freedom are illusory. In their world, despair rules. They aren't educated and they can't get jobs beyond the most menial. Although there are more of these low-paying jobs in prosperous times, there are never enough. In times of poor economic conditions, the availability of these positions shrinks drastically. Without jobs the poor can't earn money. Without money, they endure living conditions that are deplorable. Perhaps the worst aspect is that the affluence of others confronts them daily on television. They would like to enjoy the pleasures offered on the screen, but most can never have enough money unless they steal or deal drugs. Is it surprising that crime is rampant among the poorly educated?

The problems are cancerous and will continue until something meaningful is done. Conant's warning remains alive because the conditions have not improved. Schools in the slums, in his terminology, have deteriorated further since he wrote, intensifying the crisis, while better education remains the essential precondition to any improvement.

The letter (Chapter 4) that appeared in Ann Landers' column about a Philadelphia school graphically described the chaos that challenges school systems in large cities. Order and discipline have vanished; trying to teach in that atmosphere had demoralized the Philadelphia instructor who probably began his or her career with a positive and idealistic attitude. Youth in those schools don't even have that good fortune to start optimistically. They are disheartened about their chance of education from the beginning.

When discouraged students encounter demoralized teachers in a hopeless environment, results are foreordained. Inner-city schools spew out tens of thousands of students every year whose illiteracy would have seemed impossible outside an impoverished third world nation only a few years ago. In any advanced nation except the United States, this condition is unthinkable.

Something can be done. Despite the formidable obstacles, two reasons provide hope: the presence of dedicated teachers and the innate desire to learn.

Teachers are desperate to help students as the Philadelphia instructor made clear. The poor education of so many students, however, shows that teachers alone can't change present conditions, regardless of how hard they try. A basic alteration in present schooling practices must occur before they can succeed. When that happens, the dedication of these thousands of teachers will make a difference.

The second reason for a possible improvement in education is the innate desire to learn that is present in all young people, as I pointed out in Chapter 3. This desire can be squelched and made unproductive in stifling environments. Conditions in inner-city schools like the Philadelphia teacher described may obliterate academic attempts, but the desire still exists because it is innate.

The Present Disaster

Blame for poor learning and the environment that makes it inevitable is easily heaped on students. "If only the kids would behave, everything would be fine," goes the argument. "If students would only try, they could then learn." Youths are viewed as the culprits, and they could change schools by becoming better pupils.

Most children coming into inner-city schools can't fight against the crushing obstacles that confront them. Almost every entering pupil will quickly join in the general malaise. Otherwise they would have to oppose the whole cultural flow, and that would take unimaginable effort. Most youths wouldn't attempt it even if they knew how to do it. To expect them to fight entrenched student mores is hopeless. Schools are supposed to train and mold students, not be reformed by them; schools must create a new atmosphere.

Youngsters didn't devise the system that defrauds them of learning, but they are trapped in it and by it. Most of these students were behind the first day they entered school and never had a realistic opportunity to catch up. The schools knew their condition but couldn't provide a way for them to overcome that initial and basic weakness. As a consequence, poor education will harass them throughout their lives and will do the same to their children.

Whose fault is it? That is unimportant. Who can improve it? That is important. The kids can't do it; the teachers can't do it; not even the principals can do it by themselves. Somebody in higher authority must make the major changes that will allow children to learn. Somebody must take responsibility for providing a suitable learning atmosphere for these students.

The Future

If authorities are ever to revamp inner-city schools, they must correct one horrendous condition that now predominates in these schools: lack of order and discipline. Without these assets, no school can provide a suitable atmosphere for learning. No wish for academic advancement can ever be fostered without the obvious possibility that it can occur. Where order and discipline are lacking, learning is virtually impossible. Present remedies for poor discipline do nothing. Establishing rules does not create order; adding punishment also fails.

Size alone does not make discipline impossible, but if a large institution loses control, enough disruptive student leaders are always available to undermine any serious effort to re-impose it. Changing the attitudes of these leaders is close to impossible while they hold court in their accustomed milieu. They, too, are hopelessly behind in schoolwork and can only achieve a form of "success" by disrupting the school. They won't easily give up that sole claim to status.

Inner-city systems, as they seek necessary changes, need to study how private schools foster and maintain discipline and order. Their first advantage over public schools is that they are usually smaller, but they have an additional and more powerful asset beyond their size: they accept and enroll only students who have an interest in learning. This sets a tone for the school and gives authorities the power of peer pressure to aid discipline. When peer pressure fosters responsible behavior, other obstacles disintegrate. If peer pressure generates unruly behavior, everything is lost.

Private schools benefit from another feature: they can enforce discipline because students want to attend the school. Principals can quietly and unobtrusively keep in reserve the ultimate weapon: expulsion. If a student in a private school grossly violates discipline, the student can be expelled and must then attend the public school system. The ability to dismiss a student is a potent weapon that private school principals gain by having, though they seldom exercise it or even allude to it.

Order and discipline must be incorporated into public schools. While the major obstacle to regaining discipline is school size, even if authorities wish to build smaller schools, it will take years to accomplish. Since reestablishing order is impossible when it has been lost in large schools, means of downsizing within the present schools must be found. Students could then be offered the prospect of achieving an education. The omnipresent innate desire to learn will help some students choose an option where learning is possible when it is offered to them. If they find that they are learning they will have an incentive to remain in that environment. It also will be a stimulus for other students to go where they could learn. Public schools will then have the advantages of private schools: small size and peer pressure to behave.

Advocates of Choice maintain that the way to obtain the benefits of private schools is to allow parents to choose to send their children to non-public schools. In theory, this option is very attractive. The negative side is that sufficient numbers of private schools will never be started in inner cities to teach all students even if Choice were to be universal. Most inner-city parents would be without the financial means to use the private schools that will spring up in other parts of the cities. For this reason, Choice cannot be a complete solution for the needs of the inner cities.

As powerful as computers are, they alone cannot change inner-city education, but they can strengthen and augment a movement that has begun in a few places. Schools sometimes spin off part of their student body into minischools, within the same school building but separate from the rest of the student body. Computerized education will make this step practical in more locations and will improve the chances for success. These schools within a school will help authorities re-impose order and discipline.

Computerized education will allow students to have choices of many classes without having individual teachers for each subject. Since computerized education makes it possible to break the student enrollment into appreciably smaller groups, systems can establish minischools or learning schools with fewer students and without unrealistic expenses that small classes would have formerly required. Minimum requirements of levels of learning needed by entering students will not be an obstacle. Computers, even with the software available today, can start the educational process at the pre-reading level. Students will need only the wish to get an education and the willingness to try, while separated from many current obstacles.

Parents and students could be notified of the beginning of a new minischool. Parents and child will both have to be agreeable. Participation will be completely voluntary, and parents might have to agree to waive some legal rights. Certain parents and students will immediately opt for an environment more conducive to learning. The enticing cachet of computers will be a powerful impetus for students to want to be in this type of school. Pupils will, therefore, enter with at least the beginning of a suitable attitude. They will be aware that acceptable behavior is a requirement to remain. The public establishments could use the same carrot-stick technique of private institutions. Learning by computers is the carrot that will appeal to the innate desire. Gross violations of discipline will not be tolerated, and infractions of the disciplinary code will result in the stick: a return to the regular school. Small schools with only students who wish to be there will create a totally different environment: one in which learning can take place. Discipline among those students will be mandatory just as in private schools. In that atmosphere, the demonstrated ability of computers to make learning enjoyable will be a sustaining force.

With computerized education, teachers will be working in a totally different ambience from the one that now oppresses them. They will be guiding students who have an incentive to behave and to learn. They will be facilitators of learning and will have time to provide the guidance and encouragement that will be important for many inner-city youth.

Students will have another asset that is unavailable today: the sense of success and achievement that accompanies computerized education as outlined in Chapter 12. Accomplishment is important for all students but crucial for inner-city youths. Kids who start behind and fall continually further back cannot have had much success. These children, for the first time in their lives, will succeed in an academic activity. Teachers can build upon these accomplishments.

It is possible that a minischool could be located outside the main school when discipline has degenerated to an extreme degree. Community centers will provide possible locations. Many compromises are possible. Only the establishment of a learning environment where kids can learn is important.

An almost automatic source of new pupils for "learning schools" will be pupils entering the school. Every year a new class begins. Schools and children will profit if these pupils are offered the opportunity to attend a school where they can learn before they become enmeshed in the crippling educational surroundings of an establishment without order and discipline. Although loath to admit it, most kids prefer order and discipline in their lives, and many will choose that option if it is available. One successful minischool could be the forerunner of many more. One success could be duplicated innumerable times. It could mark the beginning of the radical changes needed in inner-city schools because of the inherent replicability of computerized education.

A change of this magnitude may be criticized as impractical and utopian. Critics could protest that the plan might fail, a usual and convenient objection to anything that is new and untried. Obviously, outcomes cannot be guaranteed without a trial. What is known is that the present system absolutely does not and cannot educate students. Moreover it has been proved that computerized education has been able to educate at-risk students in other locations.

Another objection might be raised. If students who want to learn are transferred, only those students who most despise formal education will remain, and the condition of the main school will be worse. Anyone suggesting that difficulty should evaluate it realistically. Inner-city schools are terrible today, and it would be difficult for them to get much worse by moving some students. Moreover, eventually it will be possible to change many of those students who most renounce learning today. Some could gradually be led to want an education, especially if they found that transferees were both learning and enjoying it. Despite their present attitudes, they still have the same innate desire to learn.

Something radical must be tried in the inner-city school systems. Without computerized education that will allow multitudes of smaller schools, probably no way can be devised to make inner-city schools into educational institutions instead of unstable and dangerous temporary dumping grounds for huge numbers of unhappy and delinquent youth. The present system has failed utterly to provide the necessary education, and no change is in sight without a drastic overhaul. Students are treated unfairly if authorities keep them in a school where learning is impossible. They should have the opportunity to receive a better education. Computers offer the best possibilities, perhaps the only possibilities. Obviously, the lives of millions depend upon finding a solution.

Chapter 27

Inclusion

Sally Brown is thirteen, blond with a cute nose and an engaging smile. She's entered puberty. Boys and dances and parties are on the minds of most girls her age, but social affairs are not part of Sally's life. She is seriously handicapped and her life is different. She lacks the control of movements of her upper extremities that most people have. Her arms sometimes jerk haphazardly and she can't speak clearly. When other people see Sally, they often don't know how to react. They don't blame her, yet there is hesitancy, perhaps even fear, about someone so different. Sally agonizes over her condition but can do nothing about it. She'll never lose her handicap, which will be her lifelong burden.

The suffering brought by serious handicaps usually comes through no fault of those afflicted. They may have been born with a genetic defect, or may have been injured in some accident that might have befallen any of us but happened to them. Sally is less concerned about the philosophical meaning of why she received her handicap, than what it means to her: a life that is always unlike and apart from most others.

Although she doesn't possess a superior intellect, Sally has average intelligence and can learn as well as most children. With extra work she might be above average in some subjects. She doesn't have much incentive to work hard, however, because she sees herself as an outcast in society. Many other people see her the same way. If Sally had lived in the seventeenth century, she would have been considered retarded and a hopeless cripple. Her family would have hidden her away in shame. We today know that this treatment was not only cruel but also wasteful and inane. Consequently, authorities insist that children like

Sally go to school. They set up programs called Special Education where those with handicaps can acquire basic learning in academic subjects and sometimes in vocational skills. Nonetheless, children like Sally are still deprived. Often they interact in school only with other handicapped children. This segregation accentuates the wide chasm that separates them from students who lead more normal lives.

Ordinary children who only see Sally from a distance may easily decide that Sally is not only different but also perplexing. At least, they can't understand Sally. Consequently, they probably will feel uncomfortable around the Sally Browns or the other handicapped people with whom they never interacted during their formative years. This is a normal reaction to segregation and is unfortunate for the handicapped but also deprives children without disabilities. They don't get to meet and to know people like Sally. They never understand disabled children as other feeling, caring, hurting, loving, human beings. Thus Special Education, with all its merits, may also intensify problems of handicapped children.

Critics have found that Special Education is the root of another difficulty. School authorities have a tendency to unnecessarily increase the number of children classified as handicapped. It is often easier for schools and for teachers to segregate children with difficulties.

Unquestionably, disabled children today have advantages that their counterparts did not have in the seventeenth century, but still greater gains could be made if these children had additional contact with other children. Until recently, school authorities didn't seriously consider trying to put handicapped children into regular classrooms, an attitude not based on cruelty or lack of awareness of the emotional needs of these children but on pragmatic reasons: handicapped children had unique requirements that seemed out of place in an ordinary classroom.

In the last half of the twentieth century, numbers of disabled Americans determined to try to enter fully into ordinary American life. Many ordinary citizens supported their efforts, and the federal government joined the movement. Laws were passed and incentives provided. New public buildings had to have entrances for the handicapped. Restrooms required suitable facilities. Sidewalks needed ramps where they crossed a street. Some public buses added means for the crippled to enter. Speakers were often accompanied by sign language translators for the hearing impaired. Traffic signs sometimes had sound for the visually impaired. These were expensive changes but relatively easy to accomplish. Bringing all handicapped people, not just the crippled, the blind or the deaf, into society is immeasurably more difficult. Problems abound and solutions are evasive.

Advocates for the disabled felt that removing children from segregated Special Education classes would be advantageous, and that became one of their goals. Several laws were passed including *The Individuals with Disabilities Education Act*, which requires that all children be educated in the least restrictive environment. There are many questions about the meaning of "least restrictive environment" and how it should be applied to a particular child. Nonetheless, that is an objective that all schools in America today must strive to attain.

After these laws passed, a new movement began in schools to which the name "Inclusion" was given. The underlying objective was to have all or most handicapped children included in regular classes rather than being in a separate section only with other handicapped children.

Almost everybody can agree that the goal is theoretically worthwhile and beneficial. When disabled children are included in mainstream classes, students with disabilities and those without all gain. Disabled children can begin to see themselves as part of society. Students without handicaps, who need to learn to accept both themselves and others, can become better educated about those who are unlike themselves.

Conflict Among Ideals

In a suburb of San Francisco, California, in a school that prides itself on being among the leaders in educational reforms, Jane Robinson instructs seventh graders. She became a teacher because she wanted to help children learn and progress, and she is strongly behind the several innovative changes that the school board has begun in recent years. She hasn't had much contact with Sally Brown who is in the Special Education section in her school, but she agrees that Sally and other handicapped children should be given extra help—as much help as possible.

When the principal of the school tells Ms. Robinson, however, that Sally Brown will now become a member of her Social Studies class, idealized theory suddenly competes with pragmatic reality. This instructor, despite her love of children and her desire to help, hesitates to have Sally in her class. While Sally Brown is gaining, other members of the class may suffer. Ms. Robinson has her hands full now. She knows that there are several students in her class who already need extra help and she can't squeeze out enough time for them. Sally will take more of her attention, and her present students will receive less. Ms. Robinson feels that as good as a less restrictive environment would be for Sally, it also will impinge on the rights of other class members. She objects to Sally coming to her class.

Thus the struggle for Inclusion faces a serious and honest obstacle from a very sincere person. Jane Robinson still wants Sally to succeed, but the rights and needs of her other students are likewise important. Today's crisis with huge numbers of children falling behind accentuates the problems.

Moreover, Inclusion in present classes is not always an unmitigated boon for handicapped children. When they have difficulty keeping up in the mainstream classes, more attention is focused on their handicap. This is one reason many parents of disabled children oppose full Inclusion.

Sometimes an attempt to offset the objections to Inclusion is made by having a Special Education teacher sit beside and aid the handicapped child in the regular class. This solves some difficulties but may create additional ones. Other students are made even more aware that this child needs extraordinary help. Moreover, other students that the Special Education teacher might have helped may be deprived of the necessary attention, and there is never enough money to supply sufficient numbers of Special Ed teachers to help every child individually.

Inclusion and Computerized Education

Many difficulties brought about by Inclusion in today's schools will disappear if computers teach all students. Handicapped children can be educated in a least restrictive environment without interfering with the rights of others.

That foundation of much of the value of computers in education, individualized instruction, will be the key element. Students will be together in all classrooms with consequent interaction that will allow each child to meet and know the other children. No student's learning, however, will be hindered by the needs or difficulties of any other pupil. Moreover, the weakness of those handicapped children who are also slower in learning, for any reason, will not stand out. Only the Leader Teacher will be fully aware of how rapidly or how slowly the child is progressing in schoolwork.

Beyond the individual instruction, the unequalled patience of computers will be a boon for the education of handicapped children. That forbearance will assist them to learn as rapidly and as effectively as is possible with the least trauma to their psyche and damage to their self-esteem.

Handicapped children also will gain a familiarity with computers, machines that will aid them throughout their lives. Computers can offset many of their infirmities as no other machine can do. They will understand early that a computerized society need have fewer fears for them than a world without computers, due to the technical adaptability of the machines.

This adaptability will begin to aid them in their school years. For example, Sally Brown has difficulty controlling the movement of her tongue and arms, but her lower extremities are not affected. She could use her computer easily and effectively with her foot directing a mouse to control the keyboard. She might not type as fast as other children but well enough to complete successfully her education in the mainstream class. Her enhanced self-confidence will provide her with a different view of her future life.

If Sally Brown could not speak at all, she could learn to manipulate the computer to make it speak for her. If Sally were completely paralyzed, she could be trained to use only her eye movements, or any muscle that she could move, to operate the computer. Even sucking and blowing air, which any person must be able to do to live, can be used to make a computer function. Although these adapted machines are only in their infancy, it is possible that they will alter the lives of the handicapped perhaps more than that of any other group of people. With computerized education, handicapped children will enter this new world at an early age.

Special Education teachers will still be needed for handicapped children just as teachers will remain essential in all education. They will be Leader Teachers and their training and creativity will help find new ways of aiding these children to become continually more involved in the full academic schedule.

Sally Brown, who faces a difficult life under all conditions, will have her obstacles lessened with computerized education. She will be a member of mainstream classes with the benefits from that position. Perhaps most importantly, as she interacts with other students, they will begin to understand what a sincere, human and lovable person is Sally Brown.

Chapter 28

Other Nations

*I*n 1993, Somalia, tiny and impoverished, managed to frustrate the most powerful nation on earth. This bizarre tale began in 1992 when graphic TV pictures of suffering and malnutrition rampant in a small section of eastern Africa appeared on news broadcasts in the United States. Americans were horrified by the effects of starvation, particularly when the victims were babies and children. Voices were raised demanding or imploring help. With the approbation of a large part of its citizenry, the American government joined with the United Nations and sent troops to try to rescue Somalia's people from the ravages they were undergoing. It was a humanitarian gesture with little or no self-seeking. After a few weeks, the efforts seemed to be successful. TV pictures showed Somali children becoming better fed and the effects of lawless bands of roaming thugs diminishing.

Then this picture, which appealed to people everywhere, of the power of wealthy nations saving lives in a grateful third world country suddenly fell apart. TV now brought a new spectacle. The Somalis were shooting the supposed benefactors and dragging the dead bodies of American soldiers through the streets. Viewers of these scenes in homes around the world were appalled and perplexed. The unexpected and violent reactions in the very people they were trying to help indicated their efforts were apparently unappreciated. They had thought that the Somali people would realize that the foreigners were achieving what they had set out to do and what everybody wanted: feed people and save lives.

Those who were puzzled by this quick turn overlooked an important element: Somalia is not a democracy. A small group had controlled it, and most ordinary people had nothing to say about what happened in daily events. Without some form of democracy, most citizens can't influence what occurs. A few powerful tyrants can control everything. In Somalia these were petty warlords, and their wishes were not necessarily those of the majority of people. These leaders had prospered while misery had been rampant in this impoverished nation. They did not want their fiefdoms destroyed.

They and their few henchmen soon began again to exercise their power, which had been briefly hidden when the foreign troops entered. As these despots once more prevailed, there was no opportunity for the ordinary people to have their desires heard or acted upon. Citizens of Somalia might prefer peace, might prefer to be fed, might prefer to live, but their ideas are irrelevant under a non-democratic form of government. Without democracy, wishes of common citizens matter little.

The solution should be easy: set up a democracy and let the people decide what they want. Since most Somalis would benefit from democracy, they should quickly opt for that form of government if given the opportunity. Unfortunately for most people in Somalia and for the foreigners who wanted to help them, it is impossible, at the present time, to set up a democracy there. The major obstacle may sometimes be overlooked: the nation has little education.

When the United States in the eighteenth century was laying the foundation for its new venture of government by the people, Thomas Jefferson warned of a danger: democracy could not succeed without an educated citizenry.[1]

His ideas are as valid today as when he wrote them. Neither Somalia nor any other uneducated third world nation can have democracy until that nation has education. Without democracy, the warlords will continue to rule. Education does not guarantee democracy but makes it possible and probably inevitable.

The United States has a similar but potentially more difficult problem just a few miles away in the nation of Haiti. People there had attempted to establish a democracy. They had an election. They chose a president by ballot. Democracy had made a start, but it ended abruptly. The president was forced to flee, and hope of a republic became faint. The United States faced a dilemma: send in troops and re-impose the president, or allow the military in Haiti to rule. Troops were sent in, but a real and permanent solution is not possible because the underlying problem in Haiti is the same as in Somalia: vast numbers of citizens are uneducated.

In Somalia, the United States could and did simply withdraw its troops and leave. Not much was lost from the American viewpoint. The answer is not that simple in Haiti because of the geographical location. It is only a few miles away from the United States. That distance is close enough for rickety boats to make the crossing and to pour out masses of these uneducated into American ghettos that were experiencing major problems before this new influx.

Haiti and Somalia are two examples of poorly educated nations that have gotten a lot of attention especially in the United States because of their accidental connection with this country. There are, however, many other equally uneducated nations in the world with rampant poverty and consequent suffering. Education is essential in these locations. A 1990 World Bank report declared "Evidence is overwhelming that education improves health and productivity in developing countries, and that the poorest people benefit the most."

Just as teaching of millions of illiterates in America requires computers, education of hundreds of millions of illiterates in Third World nations is impossible without these same machines. Just as merely placing computers in an inner-city school would not be sufficient to solve all the problems, merely placing computers in Somalia or Haiti or in other backward nations will not solve all the difficulties there. Nonetheless, just as computers open a viable means of eliminating illiteracy in the United States, they can do the same in Somalia or Haiti or in any of scores of other Third World nations.

In those countries with little education, an additional problem complicates future computerized learning: an educational infrastructure is missing and must be established. Computers, however, will make it easier to develop that infrastructure because they can be used to educate a cadre of educators quickly and more easily than ever before possible. Annabell Thomas learned to read and write at age 56 with computers. In third world nations, many talented young adults are available who can also be taught to read and write by computers. They will then form the foundation of the needed educational infrastructure that will hasten the computerized education of the balance of the nation. Although nations controlled by a small band of warlords will not seek to educate the people, countries like Haiti or Somalia where other nations become involved, can be brought to a sufficient educational level to allow representative government to take hold.

I noted earlier that when computers are proposed as a solution for America's educational difficulties, critics point to other wishful solutions that have not succeeded. In the international scene the same objection will be made. Some people thought that radio stations broadcasting lessons would solve the educational needs of children far from schools. That electronic approach helped but didn't drastically change illiteracy. Computers, however, have a feature not available on radio or TV at present. Computers allow interaction between student and machine to ensure that the student never becomes bored or lost in the lesson, both of which will destroy the learning process.

Another obstacle for computerized education in Third World countries is the language. Many of these nations not only have unique languages but they also often have more than one. It will be impossible to translate computer programs into all these idioms. The solution here is that computer programs will be written or translated into the major languages such as English, Spanish, French, or German. Children, who can learn new languages easily, can be taught to read one of the major languages by the computer as they enter school. Colonialism obviously had many serious drawbacks, but it encouraged a second language among the educated element of the population. This could be the language upon which the education of the nation would be based. Simultaneously, individual programs can be developed for each nation to teach the specific language of the region, if that is desired, but the bulk of the education would be taught in the major language the schools choose. They can thereby use the computer programs that are available in those major languages.

South Africa

South Africa is different from nations like Somalia, but education is also a major concern. While literacy is common in the white population and among some blacks, at least half of the black population is illiterate. There are interesting parallels with the demise of slavery in the United States and the abolishment of apartheid. The progress of South Africa has generated approval throughout the world. When America freed its slaves in 1863, the world was also enthralled. To make these gains permanent, education of former slaves was essential. Education of former victims of apartheid is crucial today in South Africa.

When slavery was abolished in the United States, educating all the children was probably impossible. Failure to provide effective schooling for former slaves and their dependents led inevitably to the rampant difficulties in the inner cities of the United States today. In South Africa, however, education for the nation is possible. Computerized schooling could teach every child and most adults in South Africa to read and to write. South Africa has what is lacking in Somalia: an educational infrastructure. With the portion of their population that is highly literate, South Africa can more easily supply the human personnel that will make the computer system effective.

As in America, computerized education in South Africa would have benefits both for illiterates and for those with an education. Computers could make up for the years that poorly educated children lost under apartheid but could also enhance and augment the further learning of educated school children, white and black. Nonetheless, the salient need is education of the uneducated. Wherever apartheid has left a legacy of illiteracy, computers could bring literacy.

An Additional Benefit

Computerized education in Third World nations will produce another advantage: the machines and programs will be available after the regular school day. Therefore, adults will also be able to learn from the machines after the children have left school. The final result will be dramatic. For the first time in the history of the world, computers will bring what had never before even been considered because it was utterly impossible: virtually everybody on earth will learn to read and write.

SECTION VII

CONCLUSION

Chapter 29

Commencing Computerized Education

Computerized education will mean a profound alteration in the manner in which schooling is carried on. Those affected will, therefore, have differing opinions about the feasibility and value of this new approach.

The Opponents

Resistance to change is universal and often seems almost ingrained in the human psyche. In retrospect, it seems strange that some improvements, which are valuable and widely accepted today, aroused vehement opposition when first proposed or introduced. When autos appeared, defenders of the status quo warned repeatedly of the dangers of replacing horses with machines. They were so insistent they created a still recognizable phrase, "Get a horse!"

The underlying reasons why new approaches are often in disfavor were enunciated clearly by Machiavelli:

> It must be considered that there is nothing more difficult to carry out, nor more doubtful of success... than to initiate a new order of things. For the reformer has enemies in all those who profit by the old order, and only lukewarm defenders in all those who would profit by the new order, this lukewarmness arising partly from fear of their adversaries, who have the laws in their favor; and partly from the incredulity of mankind, who do not truly believe in anything new until they have had actual experience of it.[1]

Since the proposal to supplant horses with machines aroused spirited opposition, it is not surprising that a suggestion to allow machines to do what humans have done may bring resistance that is more impassioned. The importance of education will add to the intensity as will its history of thwarting proposed changes. Long before computers, attempts to make meaningful changes met obstacles. Many new ideas have been proposed, but they have never gotten beyond the periphery of schooling and have made no substantial alteration in the system. None of these proposals was as profound as using computers to teach.

Opponents will bring up many reasons why they think computer teaching will be ineffective. Those are debatable, of course, because evidence is plentiful that computers can teach very well. Conversely, one conclusion is not debatable but will be little discussed by this opposition: the present system has proved incapable of giving a superior, or even adequate, education to millions of children.

The list of potential opponents is impressive:

1. Some teachers, without thoroughly analyzing their potential gains, may feel they must salvage the present system because they fear that proposed changes may destroy their position. An analogy may exist here with the American Medical Association and their original opposition to the establishment of Medicare. Physicians were vehement in opposing this radical innovation. Today, after the passage of many years when they have worked with Medicare, they support it unanimously even if they at times disagree with certain aspects of the program.

2. Substitute teachers, however, will be in a different category. They will no longer be needed. Their opposition to computerized education is justified from their position.

3. Many school administrators will strive to retain the present order. Lessened paperwork will mean that fewer administrators will be needed, but their big fear will be of the unknown. A change of this magnitude will have unseen consequences, which are always frightening. Hesitation or opposition of administrators is particularly troublesome because they have immense power, and they can determine what are acceptable standards in providing education. For example, they decree today that classes in which little learning takes place can be counted toward

graduation. They can also decide that other classes must follow an arbitrary pattern, based on their ideas or fears.

4. Another powerful opposition force will arise from over 1,500 schools of education that provide credits that teachers need if they wish to work in classrooms. Some of these teacher-preparation schools are excellent, some are not. Although efforts have been made to weed out the poorer schools, the task is difficult.[2] As the role of teachers shifts, schools of education and professors in those institutions must change. They will need to prepare teachers for different responsibilities. It will be a waste of time to continue many features that are prevalent today in the system of teacher education. Some faculties won't be able to make this profound switch. Schools that fear they will be threatened with extinction will, of course, be loud in rejecting a new type of education.

5. Politicians have no intrinsic interest in retaining the status quo in education, but they are influenced by votes. They will also resist major changes if they believe opponents can deliver more votes than can indifferent citizens who might favor change. Politicians, of course, hold power since they control the purse strings.

6. Some parents will oppose computer education because they fear any radical change. The opposition of these parents will be increased as they recognize that some officials—teachers, administrators, and professors of education—strongly oppose this innovation. Many citizens will believe that these recognized authorities, involved intimately in education, must know what is best.

7. Finally, computer manufacturers, although not opposed to computerized education, may give that impression because they will hesitate to act strongly. They fear that if they champion computerized education, and it doesn't come about, or until it comes about, teachers and authorities who are now responsible for purchasing computers and software will take steps to see that the offending brand is never purchased again in their school systems.

The Proponents

Despite the opposition that computerized education will generate, it will attract strong advocates from the same groups that will provide the opposition.

1. After they examine it thoroughly, I believe that most teachers will be ardent proponents of this form of education. As I have been writing this book, I have talked to a number of excellent teachers who had had no previous contact with the concept of computerized education. Universally, they opposed the idea when it was first suggested to them. After discussion, they saw that the potential advantages were magnificent. They based their approval both on the need to improve education that they all saw clearly and on the advantages to the teachers themselves. I believe that in general, the best teachers in the present system will be the ones most in favor of computerized education. They are now excellent instructors because of their many talents and dedication. Despite their stellar accomplishments today, they are still bound by the usual restrictions. Once they are freed from the innumerable menial and time consuming jobs that waste gobs of their time in today's schools, their results will be magnified. Although activities of teachers will be different in computerized education, the number of full time teachers should remain about the same.

2. Many administrators are openly dismayed by what is happening in education today and sincerely want change. They know that it must be basic and fundamental. Even some administrators who might see the advantages may cringe, however, at the possible upheaval that will occur among their teachers if draconian measures are taken. They need to know that serious changes can happen without bringing havoc to present teachers trained in the former system. The new role for teachers that will evolve in computerized education can be gradual, provided the basic change allowing computers to teach is implemented. In the Florida at-risk programs a teacher is present in every classroom but does not do the customary teaching. These are capable teachers with a history of success. They discover that facilitating the learning of stu-

dents in computerized classrooms is pleasurable, rewarding, stimulating, and satisfying. They can see what their pupils are accomplishing, and how they are assisting the children. Teachers will easily begin in this role. They can immediately be assigned as Leader Teachers allowing each child to have an individual guide. Thereafter, teachers will begin other activities including seminars, cooperative projects in many fields, and other new learning projects that their imaginations will develop. As administrators realize more fully that computerized education can fulfill their dreams for improved schools without working undue hardship on teachers, many will become strong supporters.

3. As for schools of education, many professors will see quickly the advantages of computerized education. They sincerely want improved education. They will understand that they must do their training differently, but they will also understand that they will be able to make the necessary changes. These professors know that if schools did not exist and they had the opportunity to establish them, they would never develop the present system where students who could learn spend twelve years and don't learn.

4. Parents, as they understand the potential of computerized education, will favor it. They already opt for adding computers, even though the present use adds little to the worth of education. One great advantage of discussion of computerized education may be that many concerned parents will realize that those who are controlling education are unable to overcome the problems, or they would have done so. This will lessen the fears these fathers and mothers have of going against members of the establishment who would denigrate the idea of using computers to teach.

5. Politicians are aware of the difficulties in education today. As public sentiment switches to favor computerized education, many politicians will become ardent backers of the new format.

6. Students, themselves will be another group that would select computerized education. Wherever and whenever computers are used in education today, the children love them. If they were offered a choice,

they would choose computers by an overwhelming margin. Adults, however, will make the final decisions, not the children.

Bringing Change

How will it be possible to bring computerized teaching into mainstream education? Although open discussion of the subject by all sides, proponents and opponents, is essential, the main force behind the appearance of full computerization will be the intrinsic worth of the system. This is the reason that advanced technology has been able to triumph in other industries that faced initial opposition, the reason that in spite of loud and vehement repetition millions of times of the value of getting a horse these animals are seldom found on today's interstate highway system. Just as it is now obvious that transportation by horses was doomed when autos made their appearance, future generations will look at education in the same manner. The old system was doomed when personal computers appeared. The only question is how long will it take.

Strong opposition will continue for a period of time just as defenders of horses were vehement in their antagonism to bypassing their accustomed and beloved animals. Powerful forces, positive and negative, are at work in American society today and these may hasten the process. A strong negative force that I mentioned in Section I is criminal activity. Ordinary citizens will eventually become aware that crime will not decrease appreciably without better education for the millions of youths that now leave schools overwhelmed and despairing. These same citizens will someday realize that the present system is utterly incapable of bringing improved schooling. They will also begin to see that computers, properly employed, could eliminate illiteracy and revamp education, two goals they ardently desire.

Another potent but positive force in America today is the strong push by proponents of Choice. I have earlier expressed my misgivings about this option as a total solution to the difficulties in today's system. Nonetheless, the many influential supporters of the concept will have an impact. They are earnestly searching for answers and computerized education with its manifold advantages will sometimes be considered.

The final decision about Choice will be left to voters in some locales. This may indirectly create another assist for computerized education. Choice will be seen as a threat to unions because they may not be included in these new schools. This possible eventuality together with the benefits that teachers and students will gain from computerization might encourage union leaders to improve education by supporting the new approach before voters act.

Although home-schoolers may not have enough power to force the issue, they will be able to take advantage of it when it is available. For those parents who wish to have their children learn at home, computerized education will be ideal. These guardians will have the opportunity to provide even broader education than they can do now, and the system will allow them more time to enhance their child's advancement. Other parents who might wish to employ this form of education but now hesitate to do so will find many present obstacles lessened. I expect home-schoolers to take advantage of computerized education very quickly.

Charter schools may offer the most fertile ground for the beginning of full use of computerization. Parents start these schools because they want improved schooling for their children, and innovation is usually an important part of their thinking. When they study the inherent value of computerized education, they will want their children to partake in its benefits. As the Charter school movement continues to expand, its influence on all schooling will also increase.

Making the switch to full use of computers cannot happen immediately, just as the change to autos required time. A whole system of roads had to be created from virtually nothing, refineries were essential, countless gas stations had to be built, a means of repairing the very unreliable horseless carriages was essential, and so on. It probably seemed like a hopeless undertaking to many people in 1899 just as computerization of schooling seems like a hopeless and utopian dream to many today. The Chinese proverb "A journey of a thousand miles begins with the first step" is applicable. The advent of the age of autos began slowly, and similarly, it is not essential that all or even most of the advantages of computerized education be put in place immediately. In the beginning it is not even necessary to involve all students or even a large proportion of them. A slow start is better than no start at all and will suffice to show what is possible.

The main obstacles to even a small beginning are securing suitable software, alleviating the fears of teachers, and convincing parents to entrust the instruction of their child to a computer. Parents will most likely be the least part of the problem. They are almost universally in favor of greater use of computers in the education of their children.

Teachers, and their unions, will need assurance that their numbers will not be decreased. This will have to be done by school boards. Human teachers will remain essential in computerized education although their duties must change. With the acquiescence of their unions, some teachers will be eager to try the new system that will allow them great latitude to exercise their creativity. These will become Leader Teachers for children in the computer classes, and they can begin to develop workshops and seminars for small groups of these students.

Securing the software will be difficult, but progress is being made. Some present programs can be used or adapted, and small companies are beginning to develop others. Software is now available that can teach children to read or to improve the reading of those who are behind. That is an obvious place to begin since illiteracy is so detrimental both to its victims and to the schools that must attempt to teach them. These initial steps will grow just as the requirements for the advancement of autos grew: roads were slowly built, mechanics were trained and gas stations were set up.

Certainly, enough software will soon be available to make a start, to take the first steps on the thousand-mile journey. Companies producing software will be eager to supply the market once the beginnings have been made, and the concept of computerized education has been accepted.

Even one class would be sufficient in any school to try the program. Each child would need an individual computer at all times, but it would not be necessary to have them all connected by a network, nor that all programs be downloaded from a central computer as will eventually be done. Many other future advantages can also be delayed. For example, abolishment of grades is an ultimate benefit, but is not necessary at the outset. Children could remain in their class and could be tested periodically with standard tests to assure that they were ahead of what could be expected of those in traditional classes. A short period of ordinary testing could be arranged at the beginning of the year so that children could be provided with whatever remedial software is needed. Leader Teachers can become involved in finding acceptable software that will help children who are behind make the necessary advancements. For students who are advanced, software could be found to keep them intrigued as they more quickly complete the standard curriculum for whatever grade they are in.

When children make much greater gains in the computerized classes even with the inherent shortcomings of a trial program, authorities will find ways to make the programs more widely available. The process can be gradual, as it was while horseless carriages proved their merit. The final results will be similar. Nobody today suggests going back to horses. In future years it will seem equally nonsensical to suggest returning to the practices of schools in the pre-computer era.

Chapter 30

Answering Objections

*T*he arguments against computerized education that were put forward in Chapter 6 have been answered over the course of this book. The answers will be summarized here.

How could a machine do what Miss Smith did for me in the fourth grade?

Machines cannot duplicate many effects of gifted teachers like Miss Smith. Computerized education will provide more time for Miss Smith to do what she alone can do in education because computers will relieve her of the menial tasks such as providing information to students, correcting tests and keeping current on piles of paperwork. I have emphasized how teachers will be able to aid pupils, especially in Chapters 18, 19, and 20.

Machines will break down, and students will be left with nothing to do.

Malfunctioning machines are not a major problem today and will become even less frequent as computers become ever more perfected. For the rare occasions that a machine fails, the computer of an absent pupil can be used. Machines will be tied in with the central computer where records and information will be kept. The worst mishap that could happen will be that a student must start again where he or she began at the beginning of the day's lesson.

A main computer serving the whole school could fail. That disaster might seem to be equal to a failure of a boiler or central air conditioning system, but there is one major difference: computers make a complete backup of everything they have at least once a day or usually more often. By that, they guard themselves against major disasters. The computer hardware is the least important part of the system and could be replaced within hours. Data, which form the vital component, will be immediately copied into the new machine from the backup copy. The absolute maximum loss will be a few hours of work.

Computer programs always have bugs, and students will be left with nothing to do.

Bugs in programs will be continually reduced owing to feedback to programmers. Since programs will always be improving and therefore changing, bugs can never be eliminated completely. For those that occur, an outside expert will be contacted by telephone. This will be similar to computer installations in business today where software problems are often overcome by help from knowledgeable professionals. If the assisting expert can solve the problem immediately, little will be lost. If the outside source is also stumped the problem will be left in his or her hands, and the student will go to the lessons of another course while remaining at the same machine. Eventually, all problems can be solved.

Computers can only teach certain facts, not higher-order thinking.

This is a concern of many people who misunderstand the immense flexibility of computers. I have tried to give examples of the possibilities of computers teaching advanced thinking throughout this book but chiefly in Chapter 22.

Computers can be dangerous because of Carpal Tunnel Syndrome that affects thousands of people in offices where computers are used regularly.

Carpal Tunnel Syndrome, which makes using one's hands painful, does affect some people who use computers for typing continually for hours every day. In classrooms, students will only be at their computers between two and four hours per day and they will not be typing continually at the keyboard. They will be thinking and reading more than they will be typing.

Computers can be dangerous to the eyesight of students because of the need to read from the screen.

Students sometimes strain their eyes from reading books. Color makes reading less tiring than the old black and white screens. Reading from computer monitors does not seem to be any more dangerous to eyesight than reading from books.

Some students will deliberately manhandle the computers and destroy them.

Discipline problems will be reduced materially in computerized education schools because learning will be more enjoyable than in present schools. The experience of the schools in Florida with at-risk students indicates that wanton destruction will not be a major problem. If, in rare instances, it did take place, authorities would deal with it just as they do today.

The cost of giving every student a computer is prohibitive.

Computerized education will begin to save at least some money immediately because of elimination of substitute teachers and the need for fewer non-teaching personnel. Reduction in textbook costs will also take place. The savings resulting from better student discipline and improved morale of teachers is hard to quantify but should be substantial. There will also be ongoing lessened costs flowing from smaller neighborhood schools that will allow much less costly busing. Savings for industry, the present providers of remedial education, will be substantial. Eventually, the savings to the nation as a whole will be enormous.

A machine is unable to make the judgments that a human can make.

This statement is true. Although computers can evaluate technical points like grammar, they cannot judge the value of original ideas. Seminars, which will form a vital component in computerized education, will solve this dilemma. Evaluation and judgment of ideas will also take place through peer assessment that will be available in interchange with other students, both within and outside the school. Feedback from a variety of other students may be as beneficial as that received from only one teacher, especially if that teacher is not creative.

A machine cannot teach values.

A machine can be a channel of values because of the information that it provides to students. Many values that students learn today derive from what is taught about important issues. Knowledge about the Declaration of Independence, about events leading to it and about the personages involved in writing and ratifying it, contributes greatly to an appreciation of democratic ideals. Since computers will provide a superior education, they will be able to impart values to students. Absorption of values by pupils will also be augmented by their frequent individual meetings with the Leader Teachers and through the seminars. Some groups have always been anxious to enhance teaching of their values through openly religious schools. This will still be an available option because they will be able to hire their own human teachers. Moreover, programmers can make adaptations in software that schools can choose, just as these schools choose special textbooks today.

A machine cannot develop interaction among students.

As computerized education develops, new software will be able to develop more interaction. There is already the possibility of personal exchange being stimulated as is perhaps shown today by the interaction that takes place on the Internet. There will always be interaction among students on the local level in the time outside of classes. There will be seminars and workshops that will be more frequent and more intensive than in today's schools. A new element will be added with the contact between students in other schools through telecommunications. These interchanges will be with students who have markedly different backgrounds, since they will live in different geographical locations, including different nations.

A machine cannot give the necessary and meaningful personal attention to students.

Computers will give more individual attention to students than teachers can hope to do in today's schools. Every student will have a private tutor in the computer that teaches him or her. Computers will reward students honestly but prodigiously as the pupils advance in their studies. They will never criticize or condemn a student by words nor by "body language." Moreover, the feedback given to students will be immediate, which is of more value. Whether this attention is "personal" in a technical sense may be debated, but the effects are equally powerful. The attention given by the machine will be augmented immensely by feedback from human teachers in the individual sessions that Leader Teachers will have with their pupils. This personal attention will add an entirely new dimension to the education of many students for whom teachers do not have sufficient time today.

Students will waste time if there is no teacher to check on them.

Pupils fritter away huge amounts of time today while their teacher stands before them in classrooms. They become skilled at turning soporific classes out of their minds, and they revel in daydreams about a myriad of more interesting topics while sitting silently and passively in class. During these times they don't pay attention and they learn little. Since they do not cause a disturbance, teachers don't complain. It would accomplish little if they did. Time wasted in schools under these circumstances is immense. That can never happen in computerized education. If students do not interact with the machine for a short but specified period of time, the computer will be programmed to take appropriate steps to bring the student back to reality. Computers have an ability to stimulate and excite. Pupils will not wander off into daydreams when they are being kept busy and interested. This will be the normal condition in computerized education. The interactive features will be a powerful force to keep students working and enjoying their classes. Wasting time will become an issue much less often than in present classrooms.

Bright students will discover how to use the computers to alter and destroy the system.

If it is possible, only the brightest of the bright students will ever be sufficiently skilled to penetrate far enough into the system to alter anything. Even then, the system would not be destroyed as safeguards are built into every computer system. In setting up educational systems, programmers will have the benefit of everything that has been learned about protecting millions of other systems, many with highly sensitive material. The chances of penetration of an educational system are lower both because less incentive exists, and because few, if any, students will have both the skill and the inclination to do so.

One student will be able to take the test of another student since no human will be checking.

Today, a series of lessons with unknown results requires a test afterward to determine if the pupil has learned the material. In computerized education, the machine will be constantly evaluating and will not progress until the subject matter has been learned.

A school system with computers as teachers will turn out automatons, not warm, friendly humans.

Undoubtedly, computers alone can't turn students into warm, friendly humans. Development of human assets like "warm and friendly" requires interaction with other humans along with direction and role models. Teachers will provide direction and be role models. Moreover, they will do it better than at present because they will have much more time to interact with students when computers are doing the instructing.

Some students will be unable to use computers either through fright or incompetence and will receive no education.

Programmers can make computers user-friendly and ensure that students will be able to work with the machines. Those without much experience with computers, and who don't understand the true ease of use of present machines, usually voice fears of this type.

If computers could be teachers, schools would already be using them in that way since schools now possess millions of machines.

Use of computers has been poor in education. The citation from the Congressional Office of Technology recounted in Chapter 6 about the slow advancement of technology in schools illustrates the difficulties. The advent of computerized education will involve a gigantic upheaval for educators. Those who will be most affected seldom seek major changes. Even when they begin, new ideas are accepted only grudgingly and hesitatingly.

This condition is not unique to education. Many major industrial companies, including IBM, General Motors, and Sears, believed for years that they were making changes while the companies fell into deeper problems. Educators are the same. Whenever they make use of computers, they convince themselves that they are embracing technology. Although we know that most humans don't like change, we always think of ourselves as different. Educators have that same characteristic. Although millions of computers have been used in schools, they have seldom been allowed to do more than serve as an adjunct to teachers. That pattern merely perpetuates the status quo. It does not show what computers could do if allowed to carry out that for which they are so well equipped: to teach.

Epilogue

In Chapter 1, I started by recalling the ominous warning of James Bryant Conant in 1961. Although the scene in America's urban areas was then peaceful, he stated that the underlying lack of education was contributing to "social dynamite." His foresight, including his terminology, was eerily accurate.

In 1965 the cities began their explosions. Twenty years after Conant's prediction, the government echoed many of his concerns about inadequate learning in the document whose title, *A Nation At Risk*, expressed the magnitude of the concern. That publication generated more discussion than Conant's work, but again, no substantive changes took place. As I write in 1999, over thirty years after the forewarning of Conant, and over fifteen years after the alarm of *A Nation At Risk*, the problems and their results remain: education in the inner cities is abysmal, riots continue periodically and crime terrorizes the nation.

The present disasters that stem from inadequate education are absolutely unnecessary! Computers could remake schools just as they have revolutionized other industries and institutions. The difference is that the whole fate of the nation rests on its schools. Nonetheless, despite the consequences of inferior learning that Conant foresaw so well, education dithers along in the same pattern it has used for centuries.

Objections to effective use of computers will be rampant, as I have also tried to point out. To those who do object, I ask, "What are you going to do? What other effective ideas can you produce to solve this crisis?" Thus far, little has changed in education. It remains basically the same as when Conant wrote, and when the National Commission on Education issued its foreboding. Arguably, the condition has worsened. To all those who wish to delay the effective use of computers in education I can only say, "What are you going to do? What other adequate solutions are available to solve this crisis unless you also join them with computerized education?"

Footnotes

Chapter 1 The Warning

1. Conant, James B., *Slums and Suburbs*, New York, McGraw-Hill, 1961, 2.
2. Kozol, Jonathan, *Illiterate America*, Garden City NY, Anchor Press, Doubleday, 1985, 13.
3. Florida Correctional Education School Authority, "Annual Report," Tallahassee, Florida,1990–1991.
4. New York Department of Correctional Services, "Education Intake Report," Albany, NY, 1994.
5. Berlin, Gordon and Sum, Andrew, "Toward a More Perfect Union:Basic Skills, Poor Families, and Our Economic Future," New York, Ford Foundation, 1988.
6. Allen, Jeanne Abate, *New York Times*, "What Business Can Teach the Schools", Jan 20, 1991, III, 11:2.
7. U.S. Department of Education, Office of Educational Research and Improvement,National Center for Education Statistics, "College Level Remedial Education in the Fall of 1989," Washington, 1990
8. U.S. Department of Education, Office of Educational Research and Improvement, National Center for Education Statistics, "Statistical Analysis Report: Remedial Education at Higher Education Institutions in Fall 1995, Washington, 1996.
9. Bronner, Ethan, "U.S. High School Seniors Among Worst in Math and Science," *New York Times*, February 25, 1998.
10. Ravitch, Diane, "Japan's Smart Schools", *The New Republic*, Jan 6, 1986, 11.
11. DeWitt, Karen, "Verbal Scores Hit New Low in Scholastic Aptitude Tests," *New York Times*, August 27, 1991, A1.
12. Singal, Daniel J., "The Other Crisis in American Schools", *Atlantic Monthly*, November 1991, 59–74.
13. U.S. Department of Labor, Secretary's Commission on Achieving Necessary Skills, "What Work Requires of Schools: A SCANS Report for America 2000," Washington, 1992.
14. DeWitt, Karen, "Labor Department. Outlines Job Skills Students Will Need in Future," *New York Times*, July 3, 1991, A1.
15. Miller, Krystal, "At GM, The Three R's Are The Big Three," Dow Jones/News Retrieval, 7/3/92.
16. National Commission on Excellence in Education, "A Nation At Risk," Washington, April 1983, 5.
17. ibid.

Chapter 2 Some Suggested Solutions

1. AMERICA 2000, Washington, DC, 1991, 1.
2. cited in Toch, Thomas, *In the Name of Excellence*, New York, Oxford University Press, 1991, 204.
3. Ravitch, Diane, ibid.
4. U.S. Congress, Office of Technology Assessment, *Power On! New Tools for Teaching and Learning*, OTA-SET-379,Washington, DC: U.S. Government Printing Office, September, 1988, 151.

Chapter 3 A Look at Education

1. Tomlinson, Tommy, Conference on "Hard Work and High Expectations: Motivating Students to Learn," Issues in Education, Office of Educational Research and Improvement, Washington, 1992, 1.
2. Dusek, J.R., "Do Teachers Bias Children's learning?", Review of Educational Research, 1976, 661–84.

Chapter 5 A True Solution
1. American Council on Education, *1991 Statistical Report*, GED Testing Service (Publications), Washington, DC, 1992, inner cover.
2. Grise, Phil, "First Year Status Report on Florida Districts use of the GED for At-Risk Students," Florida State University, Tallahassee, FL, 1991, 16.
3. American Council on Education, ibid.,34.
4. Kadlecek, Dale, "Paper Presented at the 2nd Annual Conference on At-risk Students," n.d.

Chapter 6 Overview of Computers in Education
1. U.S. Congress, Office of Technology Assessment, ibid., 187.

Chapter 7 Problems Confronting Teachers
1. U.S. Congress, Office of Technology Assessment, Teachers and Technology: *Making the Connection*, OTA-EHR-616,(Washington, DC:U.S. Government Printing Office, April, 1995), 2.
2. ibid., 20.
3. U.S. Congress, Office of Technology Assessment, 1988, 100.
4. ibid., 115.
5. ibid., 88.
6. ibid.,17.

Chapter 8 Problems Confronting Programmers
1. ibid., 122; see also 142-3.
2. ibid., 145.
3. Chapter 7.
4. U.S. Congress, Office of Technology Assessment, 1988, 132.

Chapter 10 Educating the Disadvantaged
1. Terman, Lewis, "Intelligence Tests and School Reorganization", *World*, New York, 1923), 27, as cited in Oakes, Jeannie, *Keeping Track How Schools Structure Inequality*, Yale University Press, 1985, 36.
2. Toch, Thomas, ibid., 123.
3. Oakes, Jeannie, ibid.; Manserus, Laura, "Should Tracking Be Derailed?" *New York Times*, IVA,14–16, November 1, 1992; Toch, Thomas, ibid., 123.
4. Brown, P. and Goren, P., "Ability grouping and tracking: Current issues and concerns," National Governors Association, Washington, 1993.
5. Manserus, Laura, ibid.
6. Bulkely, William M., "Illiterates Find Computers are Patient Mentors, *The Wall Street Journal*, November 16, 1992, B1.

Chapter 13 Using Educational Research
1. Dempster, Frank N., "The Spacing Effect A Case Study in the Failure to Apply the Results of Psychological Research," *American Psychologist*, 43(8), Bug... 1988, 627–634.

Chapter 14 Directing Multimedia
1. Fletcher, J.D., "Effectiveness and Cost of Interactive Videodisc Instruction in Defense Training and Education" Institute for Defense Analyses, Alexandria, Virginia, 1990.
2. Plato, *The Republic, Book VII*, translated by Benjamin Jowett, World Library, 1991, screen 470:646.

Chapter 15 Eliminating Prejudice
1. AAUW Educational Foundation, *How Schools Shortchange Girls*, Washington, DC, 1992.
2. Sadker, Myra, and Sadker, David, *Failing at Fairness: How America's Schools Cheat Girls*, New York, C. Scribner's Sons, 1994.

Chapter 16 Eliminating Substitute Teachers
1. Toch, Thomas, ibid., 114.
2. New York State Office of Education Performance Review, "Teacher Absenteeism in New York City and Cost Effectiveness of Substitute Teachers,"(Albany, N.Y.:State Department of Education, January, 1974). as cited in Elliot, Peggy, and Manlove, Donald, "The Cost of Skyrocketing Absenteeism," Phi Delta Kappan, 59, 4, 1997,269–271.
3. e.g., Drury, William R.,"Eight Ways to Make Sure Substitute Teachers aren't Baby-Sitters," *American School Board Journal*, vol. 175, n3, March, 1988, 51; Tracy, Sandra J.. "Improve Substitute Teaching With Staff Development," *NASSP Bulletin*, vol. 72, May 1988, 85-88.

Chapter 18 General Activities of Future Teachers
1. Plato, *The Republic, book.IV*, translated by Benjamin Jowett, World Library, 1991, scr. 240:646.

Chapter 21 Future Schools
1. Conant, James B., *The American High School Today: A First Report to Interested Citizens*, New York, McGraw-Hill, 1959, 40.
2. For a review of some of the research, see Fox, William, "Relationship Between Size of Schools and School Districts and the Cost of Education" U.S.Department of Agriculture, *Technical Bulletin 1621*, 1980.
3. For a review see Huling, Leslie,"How School Size Affects Student Participation, Alienation." *NASSP Bulletin*, 64,438, October 1980,13–18
4. Fritz Hess, Wilfred Martin, Donald Parker,and Jerry Beck, "School Size and Its Effect on Achievement and Other Educational Issues," *Chapter I of Issues in Education:A Documented Look at Seven Current Topics*, compiled by Fritz Hess et al., 1-21, 1978.
5. Montgomery County Public Schools, "Report of the Small Schools Task Force," Rockville, MD, 1973.
6. Ornstein, Allan C., "School Size and Effectiveness: Policy Implications", *Urban Review*, vol. 22, no. 3, Sep. 1990, 239–245.
7. "School Size: A Reassessment of the Small School," Eric Clearinghouse, *Educational Management*, Number 21, February 1982.
8. e.g., Stewart, Jim, et al.,"Science as Model Building", *Educational Psychologist*, 27(3), 334.

Chapter 22 Grades
1. Tomlinson, Tommy, ibid., 3.

Chapter 23 Better Thinking
1. Atwood, Virginia A. and Wilen, William W., "Wait Time and Effective Social Studies Instruction," *Social Education*, March 1991, 179–181.
2. Killoran, James, "In Defense of the Multiple-Choice Question," *Social Education*, 56(2), 106–108, February 1992.
3. U.S. Congress, Office of Technology Assessment, 1988, 49.

Chapter 24 Paying for Computerized Education

1. Chapter 1.

2. Texas Select Committee on Public Education, "Recommendations", 1984, 42.

Chapter 28 Other Nations

1. Malone, Dumas, *Jefferson and His Time*, Volume six, *The Sage of Monticello*, New York, Little, Brown and Company, 1981, xv; Jefferson, Thomas, *Writings*, New York, The Library of America, 1984, 859, (Letter to George Wythe, August 13, 1786,) 1222, (Letter to Messrs. Hugh L. White and Others, May 6, 1810,) 1226, (Letter to John Tyler, May 26, 1810,) 1248, (Letter to Alexander von Humboldt, April 14, 1811,) 1387–8, (Letter to P.S. Dupont de Nemours, April 24, 1816).

Chapter 29 Commencing Computerized Education

1. Machiavelli, Niccolo, *The Prince*, Chapter 6, Translated by Luigi Rici, New York, New American Library, 1952, 49.

2. Texas Select Committee on Public Education, ibid.

Index

About the author

Frederick Bennett received his undergraduate degree in Business Administration. When he finished, he was relieved that he would never have to be in school again. After college he began as a salesman and later established a book distribution business.

Idealism then got the better of him and he decided to change the world. The way he chose was to enter the Roman Catholic priesthood. It was back to school again and he received an STL (Licentiate in Sacred Theology) from the Pontifical University Angelicum in Rome, Italy. Returning to the U.S. he taught Greek and performed ministerial functions.

He returned to school again and received an MA in Counseling at the University of New Mexico and then a Ph.D. in Psychology from the University of Utah in 1971. After the advanced degrees, he helped set up a treatment program for clergy with alcoholism and also worked in an inner-city mental health center. It was there that he first confronted the reality that some people without education could not get a job, regardless of how much they wanted to work.

Eventually, he realized he was not changing the world and left the priesthood.

He directed public addiction treatment programs in Colorado and Florida and married a Ph.D. chemist who was an excellent teacher. Thereafter, he established, owned, and directed a group of private addiction treatment centers. He also became interested in computers and began to write programs to handle the paperwork for his company.

In 1990 he sold the business, moved to Sarasota, Florida, and began new projects. One was writing a computer program for artists, which he markets on the Internet. He also started to think seriously about the problems in education and spent several years studying the subject. His wife's background in education was of immense help. Finally, he sought to bring together what he had acquired from his studying and education, from his experience working with people at all levels, and from his knowledge of computers. The result is the book, *Computers as Tutors: Solving the Crisis in Education.*

In addition to the usual book sources,
Computers as Tutors: Solving the Crisis in Education,
can also be ordered direct from the publisher,

Faben, Inc.
(Toll Free)   **888-671-5112**
(Fax) **941-365-5472**

http://www.fabenbooks.com
e-mail: sales@fabenbooks.com

The author, Frederick Bennett, can be contacted at
bennett@fabenbooks.com